Leading for Impact
and Jennifer Schielke

In *Leading for Impact*, Jennifer Schielke crafts an inspiring narrative that intertwines faith, family, and professional excellence in a way that resonates deeply. Her wisdom goes beyond mere leadership principles, fostering a holistic approach to life's various roles. Whether you're a seasoned executive or just beginning your journey, Schielke's insights will empower you to articulate your vision, align with your team, and build a legacy of enduring success. This book is not merely a guide but a companion on your path to greatness. You'll find yourself returning to its pages time and again, drawing from its well of inspiration and practical advice. *Leading for Impact* deserves a prominent place on the bookshelf of anyone committed to positive growth and transformation.

—David L. Schreiner, PhD
President/CEO, Katherine Shaw Bethea Hospital
Author of *Be the Best Part of Their Day*

Leading for Impact explores the essential ingredients of leadership in an easy-to-understand format and provides a concrete roadmap for anyone motivated to improve their personal and professional leadership skills. The book encourages leaders to strive for excellence with integrity while being a transformative servant leader who continues to grow personally and professionally. It is an outstanding guide for leaders to stretch beyond their comfort zone and a must-read for incorporating personal faith in leadership. *Leading for Impact* is a valuable addition to the toolbox of both leaders and aspiring leaders.

—Norma Morris
Senior Director of National Philanthropy (retired),
City of Hope

In *Leading for Impact*, Jennifer Schielke highlights the profound connection between a leader's team and their own self-awareness. With this vital insight woven seamlessly throughout its pages, the book becomes an invaluable resource for aspiring leaders seeking to cultivate impactful relationships.

—David Heaps
Executive Coach and Principal at Leadering

In a world desperate for genuine leadership, Jennifer Schielke's *Leading for Impact* stands as a testament to the power of honesty, accountability, and compassion. With rare authenticity, her words hold the potential to not only reshape the way we lead, but also to reshape the world we lead in. I wholeheartedly recommend this book to anyone who believes in the transformative potential of leading with integrity. The wisdom Schielke shares doesn't feel distant or unattainable; instead, it feels like a trusted friend providing you with the guidance needed to navigate the intricate terrain of leadership while staying true to your values.

—Kelley Curtin
Senior Business Program Manager, Microsoft

The best leaders offer guidance, purpose, and motivation for teams to rally behind. They generously impart their expertise and insights to others with integrity and humility. Jennifer's new book, *Leading for Impact*, delivers a timely message that will resonate with leaders from various fields and experiences. Whether you're a CEO steering a large organization or a community leader guiding a small team, the invaluable wisdom presented in this book will equip you to lead with authenticity and a strong sense of purpose.

—Austin Lashley
Senior Vice President, Hughes Marino

Leading for Impact provides not only direction and insight as a guidebook for leaders, but also a compelling storyline into Schielke's personal leadership journey. Integrity, remaining true to yourself, and growth as both an individual and a leader are consistent themes and "Sparks of Truth" throughout the book. These messages offer direction to any leader who is ready to be vulnerable in their approach to growing as a strong yet thoughtful leader.

—Taylor Reed
Human Resources Consultant, Asure Software

Leading

FOR

Impact

JENNIFER SCHIELKE

Leading

FOR

Impact

**THE CEO'S GUIDE TO
INFLUENCING WITH INTEGRITY**

Advantage | Books

Published by Advantage Books, Charleston, South Carolina.
An imprint of Advantage Media.

ADVANTAGE is a registered trademark, and the Advantage colophon is a trademark of Advantage Media Group, Inc.

Printed in the United States of America.

10 9 8 7 6 5 4 3 2 1

ISBN: 978-1-64225-762-5 (Paperback)
ISBN: 978-1-64225-761-8 (eBook)

Library of Congress Control Number: 2023916279

Cover design by Matthew Morse.
Layout design by David Taylor.

This publication is designed to provide accurate and authoritative information in regard to the subject matter covered. It is sold with the understanding that the publisher is not engaged in rendering legal, accounting, or other professional services. If legal advice or other expert assistance is required, the services of a competent professional person should be sought.

Advantage Books is an imprint of Advantage Media Group. Advantage Media helps busy entrepreneurs, CEOs, and leaders write and publish a book to grow their business and become the authority in their field. Advantage authors comprise an exclusive community of industry professionals, idea-makers, and thought leaders. For more information go to **advantagemedia.com**.

"Not to us, LORD, not to us but to your name be the glory, because of your love and faithfulness."

—Psalm 115:1

CONTENTS

I'm a success today
because I had a friend
who believed in me, and
I didn't have the heart
to let them down.

—ABRAHAM LINCOLN

At a time when culture desperately seeks to promote group identity, be the one to define who you are for yourself, in a manner that holds certainty and meaning. Trust yourself to find the foundation intended for you. Use it to serve your purpose well and to serve others generously. Own your past, embrace the present, and celebrate your future. Your impact is *your* responsibility alone, and being you is a liberty that *only* you get to experience in its fullness. An outworking of that solid foundation in each of us is the privilege of influencing others with integrity and leading for impact.

My purpose is to *uphold all that God has entrusted to me.* That means to be a good steward over people, talents, and the opportunities and challenges life promises to deliver. It is an honor to engage in the professional lives of men and women, and I count myself fortunate to be able to both influence and learn from each of them. I am encouraged by witnessing those who are *active* in their leadership journey and who are empowered by the dignity intended for them.

In a world full of people, relationships matter. Regardless of how innovative technology becomes, relationships matter. To foster those human connections, it is crucial to assume good intentions and be interested in the individual stories of others. Rather than be self-consumed, place others before you. That also means being vulnerable and open, willing to share both your successes and failures, and inviting others to engage in that same way. Guard your heart, open your mind, and give of yourself freely yet wisely. Teach others what you do and share your knowledge. Then you, yourself, must do what you teach, and be a willing student. The journey isn't just about celebration; it's the reality of including the stumbles and falls that come before the rise. Own your journey, all of it—good, bad, and ugly. Onus gives way to integrity.

I am a fallible human, but that does not deter me from striving for excellence in everything that I do. I know what I believe and who (and whose) I am. That is my identity and worth. It is *my* immovable foundation.

For I am convinced that neither death nor life, neither angels nor demons, neither the present nor the future, nor any powers, neither height nor depth, not anything else in all creation, will be able to separate us from the love of God that is in Christ Jesus our Lord.

—Romans 8:38–39

Where I am now isn't because I merely dreamt of arriving here one day; it is where I've been led through intention, action, humility, and gratitude. I am pleased to share a glimpse into my leadership journey to enable you to find a connection point to your own story. This isn't meant to be about me. It's meant to be a launching point for your own leadership growth. This is not about being afforded a title or a position you think you somehow deserve above everyone else. This is about your whole self—perhaps it's especially about the parts that you don't want to look at. *You are the strongest influencer of your life and your leadership.* Reflecting on our character, the whole of who we are—of leadership—is about finding meaning in our stories, so I'll begin with mine.

There is so much to appreciate and to *balance* from where I began and where I stand now. *Simplicity, resilience,* and *contentment* are the words that come to mind. I grew up on the beautiful island of Kaua`i with little money but always had a shelter over my head, clothes on my back, and food on the table. I had enough. Like many in my generation, most of my childhood was spent outdoors playing until dark. My fondest memories are of fishing, dancing hula, watching football, studying hard, working harder, and just being grateful for everything.

My family faced its share of challenges and hardships. Brokenness is real for all people, to varying degrees, in different ways, and at different times. We lived paycheck to paycheck with both parents working, sometimes multiple jobs. I worked through high school and college; even with a highly sought-after job in my field, the first few years were made of constant choices and sacrifices to get out of debt. I am grateful that nothing was handed to me; I am better for it. The truth is, hardship lends its own perspective, builds resilience, and fosters gratitude and contentment.

Regardless of my private home instability and brokenness, I still had a perception that I was more fortunate than most, and I believed that I was loved by both my parents, to the best of their abilities. I witnessed firsthand how hard work produced opportunities and financial security. Life circumstances taught me early on how to be a productive, contributing member of society. Academic accolades filled me with the satisfaction of achievement. Standing on my own two feet, standing on solid ground, fueled my courage to leave everything I knew and start a new life on my own.

The traditional and simple aspects of life still motivate much of what I do as a person and as a leader. Relational connections don't have to come with extravagance, especially if they are rooted in genuine interest and good intentions. With all the distractions in the world, I prefer to sink back into quiet simplicity to recharge. Knowing what you need, and *doing* just that, is so critical to contentment, achievement, and supporting your team(s). It's important to refuel your leadership tank. Even in putting others first, you must maintain a solid foundation for yourself. Doing so enables you to pour into others more and take them further—truly empowering you to be a better leader.

My strength comes from my own experiences—who I am, how I was raised, who influenced me, and who I *chose* to be influenced by—while knowing that I am fearfully and wonderfully made[1] with purpose and impact. Today, these values are carried into the company I cofounded, Summit Group Solutions, LLC, and the adjoining teams that I have the privilege to lead and serve. Fostering shared values into what you do enhances your life and the lives of others. It enables you to bring your whole self to every circumstance and invites others to do the same.

I channeled anything negative or broken at home—or broken within myself—and repurposed these challenges into a launching pad to get to where I wanted to go. To say that I did it alone would be a fallacy. I recognize how very fortunate I've been to always have someone who believed in me—perhaps more than I did myself—at every stage of my life. Teachers and professors, bosses and colleagues, friends and family, mentors and peers, whether I perceived them

---

1   Psalm 139:14

as good or bad, are part of the same tapestry and deserve the same gratitude.

Mentorship and encouragement can come from many different sources. My most impactful time of growth took place at a global training center where I served in ministry. This experience centered me in my faith, allowed me to live out commitment with diligence, taught me compassion, and showed me the true meaning of leadership. I was pushed beyond my comfort zone, over and over again, while being given opportunities that I will treasure for eternity. Those years spent intently in ministry, service, and surrender left me feeling more purposed than I'd ever experienced in my life.

I was not equipped to step into all the places I was called to go, but I still went—telling myself, it's not about my comfort and confidence; it's about my need to grow and the impact that ensues. Not about me but the purpose I serve. *Surrender*—I'd assumed it to be the opposite of fearlessness, but now, fearlessness and surrender are inseparable to me. I surrendered to the calling placed before me, trusting God to equip me and use me. I needed to get out of the way to be an effective leader and true to the purpose intended for me. From then on, the responsibility to be mindful of my own influence (and influencers), my integrity (character), humility, and gratitude were at the forefront of all that I did and shaped who I would become.

The reality I adopted was that it's not about me. I transitioned past *ego-driven* fearlessness, which is focused on self, to a *humbled* fearlessness (servant leadership), which is focused on others. Thus, surrendering of self to be fully outward-facing and void of selfish ambition or desires. Ego-driven leadership—without the surrendering of oneself—leaves the personal and relational elements of impactful leadership aside and even becomes a barrier to learning and growing due to the unwillingness to look inward, to receive, and to embrace areas of vulnerability. Ego breeds pride and arrogance, which lacks integrity, because one is driven toward what one wants rather than what is right, or even, what one really needs. Surrender is courageous because it is counter to that survivor instinct—it isn't culturally taught as a strength. I had to be fearless in my surrender to fuel a willingness to see both my strengths and my weaknesses—those areas where I had the opportunity to refine. That commitment to self-improvement affords an experience of vulnerability, which in turn is a connection point to others and a sharpening of yourself and your character, which comes back to the spirit of courage.

Living humbled, yet fearless, gave me a genuine sense of celebration for each and every individual (through the good, bad, and ugly). Listen, no one is perfect. Not one of us. I don't care who you are or who you strive to be; we all have ugly moments. I've had more than my fair share! Yet, we discover grace in how we reconcile, in how we reach out, come to the table with honest dialogue, and face our fears. We intentionally apply our learning and press onward. I am not greater than anyone else, but neither is another greater than me. I believe in the dignity and worth of each person while upholding others to the value and worth intended for them.

Leading for Impact is meant to meet you where *you* are and to inspire you to be intentional and purposeful in your field of work. As you read with a desire to see something new, to boldly grab hold of and transform yourself (and therefore your teams), my genuine hope is that you are inspired to execute on your leadership development and team empowerment.

The times we are in now overwhelm us with so much noise—distractions, pressures, and exposure—that it seems impossible, even intimidating, to make discerning and wise decisions. Our challenge and our privilege as leaders are to be bold with our ethics, values, intentions, and even our shortcomings. I encourage you to look deep within yourself to see things outside the scope of "traditional" leadership. It's more important than ever to make decisions geared toward positively impacting the people influenced by your guidance, centered in what you *believe*—what you *know* at your core, with positive intention and integrity.

Our call is to step up and create a strong path forward. Who we are as *individuals* must be in harmony with who we are as leaders. If you bring your whole self to everything that you do, you will be working through transformative leadership principles. This approach takes your influence to the next level. The saying "You get out what you put in" rings true, and I believe that you cannot take people further than you yourself have gone. We each lead in different spheres of our lives. We all have different gifts, passions, and visions of success. For me, success is being a faithful steward over all that has been entrusted to me and that includes—perhaps culminates with—the people I have the honor to serve and lead.

Leading for Impact is for those who desire a deeper connection to people-based, values-based management—those who want to build a team, *keep* a team, and create lasting success. It's for those who are boldly willing to step into uncertainty and reap the rewards of hard work, self-reflection, and being trustworthy—that is, consistent application of your value foundation regardless of outside influences. Whomever you are as you start this journey, your impact is broader and deeper than you realize. Never has it been more important for us to grow in humility and celebrate generously. Be the leader to influence with integrity and lead for impact—not for your own glory and accolades but for those who look to you for what is to come. Be the spark, the light, and the leader to follow.

Introduction Spotlight

A leader for impact fosters success through transformative relationships.

SPARKS OF TRUTH

- A leader controls their own life and leadership.

- Leaders have the privilege and responsibility to positively influence others.

- Humbled fearlessness is rooted in a *selfless* focus rather than ego-driven self-focus.

- Humility fosters transformation, while arrogance and pride are barriers to growth.

- Businesses can achieve financial success while also investing in their people.

PROMPTS FOR IMPACT

- Share your leadership story.

- How has your leadership transformed over the past year?

- How do you show your investment in the people you lead?

NOTES

....
....
....
....
....
....
....
....
....
....
....
....
....
....
....

Whatever you are, be a good one.

—ABRAHAM LINCOLN

CHAPTER ONE

The Leader You Are

leader: a person with commanding authority or influence.

Leaders in history are many—some to be admired, some to be forgotten, and none without a trail of mistakes that rival their victories. We are no different in our own leadership stories. You are exactly where you've chosen to be, with obstacles along the way. Accept this awareness in its fullness. You know where you've been, where you are, and where you want to go. The past has served its purpose in shaping you for such a time as this. The present allows you to take in the full appreciation of who you are and what kind of a leader you have become. The future holds unlimited potential to be the leader you were chosen to be. Be accountable to this future, ignite the fire within, and invite its refining power as you become a leader to celebrate. Leadership enables you to grow and create a fountain of prosperity for yourself and those you lead. Be a leader of influence; be the leader you were purposed to be.

Leading for Impact encourages you to reflect and engage. It's a call to get off the sidelines and into the game. Reflect on what experiences best prepared you to lead. Who influenced you the most? Who motivates you now, challenges you, and celebrates with you? My fondest memories of leadership come from early in my youth. I remember being chosen by my teachers and peers in grade school and straight through college for various leadership positions. Each experience has a different impact on ability, emotion, bandwidth, and takeaways.

My first recollection of "leading" was in second grade when I was chosen for our school's May Day court. For reference, modern May Day celebrations in Hawai'i are very special for the entire community. This annual celebration is filled with traditional symbolism and pageantry. Each island has its own cherished color and flower, as well as *mele* (songs) and *mo'olelo* (stories). When I was elected to the May Day court, we didn't have the resources to make or purchase the elaborate *holoku* gowns required, but each time, a former family who had been afforded the same privilege that I was about to enjoy came forward and graciously loaned me what was needed.

I was chosen again in fourth and sixth grades. Each time, I was honored to serve and stand in the court before the entire school and neighborhood families. The sense of honor, trust, generosity, and community has never left me. I am grateful for that. On each occasion, from elementary school and beyond, I wanted others to experience the moments I was given, to grow, to celebrate, and to give back. Leadership opportunities are all around us, and I worked very hard to uphold every position ever afforded me. At the same time, different experiences led me to understand that relationships were more important than any position or any single person alone. This realization has served me well.

More than once, I would willingly step aside to foster the growth of another, presenting them with the opportunity to flourish. My worth and level of contribution do not vary by position or title. Every role matters, and every person has an impact to make. When I jump into something, it's with everything that I have to give and nothing less. That's the success meter I have—do everything that I can under the circumstances presented, to the best of my abilities, and with a clear conscience (integrity). Leave the situation better than it was when I first found it, and honor the people I led, followed, or stood beside.

Think about the leader you are today. What do others say about your leadership—about *you*? What *values* are important to you as a leader? How do they show up in your daily interactions? The experiences you've had, the people you've met, and the decisions you've made have placed you where you are now. What strengths do you naturally possess, and what do you want to sharpen in the future? You are who you set out to become!

Fearless and *driven* are the words that are top of mind for me. Perhaps because they are both inherent in who I am as well as intentional in my devotion to excellence. I've handled more than my share of life-on-life reality. As a child of domestic violence and a leader in ministry to a broken world, I am a humbled and grateful servant. Strong determination translated itself into hard work. I didn't have academic expectations placed upon me, so I set my own bar and was driven and empowered to be an achiever. My strides were noticeable, honest, and bold. I think one reason I was constantly in leadership roles is that I was truthful and never swayed in my convictions. To the contrary, I rose to difficulty and sometimes invited challenges. The downside of that was that I lacked compassion.

Compassion, or lack thereof, seemed to be overshadowed by my drive repeatedly when I was young. I set a high standard of excellence for myself and those around me. I thought, if I lived up to those standards, it was logical that others should as well. On more than one occasion, I have been told of these "impossible standards" (even recently, if we are being honest). Enter ministry and transformative training. I realized that my desire to lead, teach, edify, encourage, and draw people away from brokenness and hurt was the untapped well-spring deep inside me that wanted to pour into others. My approach had to be reshaped and my purpose defined. This refinement is why an open mind and heart are important. Constant learning and development are critical; otherwise, you may miss the powerfully unique ways you can show up to walk alongside and lead someone else. "Start where you are. Use what you have. Do what you can" (Arthur Ashe), but constantly strive to be better!

In this day and age, you can go to the moon, the depths of the sea, or an alternate and virtual reality. The future seems limitless. Your life and leadership moments are limitless, as well. You guide it and bring it to fruition with what you do or don't do. When your professional life is complete, think about what kind of a leader you want to be remembered as, and start creating the path that gives rise to your leadership dreams. Decide what you need to do now to align how you lead, and who you are as a leader, with your vision of success and legacy.

For me, it all comes back to my own success statement (and I recommend that you have one too)—*To be a faithful steward over all that God has entrusted to me.* All people, things, circumstances, choices, and opportunities—*all that is entrusted to me.* My team knows that I am committed to our culture (living out our vision, mission, and values), and they know my personal success statement. They know my personal values because they see evidence of it, and they encourage me toward it.

We have three pillars that I established to unify us in our roles: *engaged in our value-driven culture, courageous in the pursuit of professional growth, and committed to achieving operational goals.*

I remind them that, as a company, we invest in their professional development, so I expect that they, too, invest in *their own* growth. That means coming to the table, even (or especially) in disagreement, and holding each other accountable to the pillars, our values, our vision, and their own goals. Character matters in all circumstances at all times. I expect to see evidence of their commitment to the pillars established, and I lead the charge to do the same.

I've seen teams implode because they acted apart from our values and their given roles. Some things are, in fact, absolute and essential. As a leader, it's important to know who you are and where you are going, to articulate it and to live it out with excellence—*not perfection*, but excellence.

The Learning Leader

One who is courageous in the pursuit of professional growth, for themselves and others, always achieves success.

I've seen leaders who stop growing—stop learning—and still boast of their positions and successes. Remember, you can't take others further than you've gone yourself. My corporate role calls upon me to see the potential in others and edify them, but this would be impossible if I limited *my own* development and ceased pushing my own boundaries every day. I must *want* to learn in order to inspire others to also seek that growth within themselves. Traditional leadership models and the current culture of "I" lure us to believe it stops at "I did my job"—the minimalist. Maybe it's sufficient for some, but that dismisses the potential to do so much more, such as uplifting others during the process. It's not just about you and your title; it's about those under your authority and care, and the *you* as a leader that has yet to be.

There's nothing wrong with being content in your leadership, but being complacent or entitled will hinder your leadership development and effectiveness. I've witnessed leaders who seem to have an honest desire to grow professionally but refuse to grow personally or compartmentalize the two. Imagine the heights you could reach as you keep learning—as you keep improving your whole self. If you want continued success, personal growth is an essential part of that daily achievement. Professional and personal growth are positively correlated, and they work together to launch you into a new realm of ability and potential.

I was once that person who separated—or thought that I *could* separate—the components of my life. There was the wife, mom, daughter, ministry leader, dog mom, school room parent, and then there was the corporate leader. I wore many different hats/titles and functioned differently in each space. This mindset lasted for a while, but ultimately, the isolation in each arena limited me. It was like an aspect of me was in a perpetual time-out or just missing. One day, I realized that the same complete me had to flow through everything. We're taught to compartmentalize parts of our lives, but genuine growth reaches all components of you—as a parent, coach, friend, CEO, and so on. Every part builds on and complements the other. Our whole self is part of our leadership. Don't strip yourself of the talents and gifts you hold.

I remember a time when the director at my children's preschool stopped me and said she knew who I was—meaning she could see I was the same person whether in front of her, at work, and the like. My decisions and actions were not influenced by where I was or who I was with but rather by my solid foundation. She shared how refreshing it was to see someone who didn't pretend or set different rules in different spaces. My consistency allowed her to have confidence in how I would handle any given situation—it would be the same whether in front of her desk, in a hallway, at home, or in a grocery store.

The director commended my commitment to my children's development through discipline, truth, and affirmation undeterred by anything or anyone in my environment. It was true, my husband and I raised our children to protect them and teach them right and wrong. My measure has never been based on what someone else thought or did. In fact, my kids understand it would be worthless to say "so-and-so's parents do this" or "my teacher said that." My, and of course, my husband's, parental authority superseded all else. The blessing and parental right and responsibility were given to me by the grace of God, and I hold that in the highest regard. No one can take that from me.

It pleases me still that others see me for my true self. I was the same leader (in this case, parent). No matter the circumstance or where I was, I upheld my role. That consistent expectation, even if it means consequences, establishes security and reliability, which is also important for an inclusive and safe environment. When people know what to expect from you, when you've established a pattern of support, they are more likely to come to you and rely on you. You leave them with less uncertainty and build greater trust.

Perhaps pieces of you shine brighter or are used more frequently in some environments, while other areas are a bit more of a challenge.

For instance, you command the household with grace but run on a short fuse at work or vice versa. Still, that's the same *you*. I view this patchwork of life experiences as an opportunity designed to practice my strengths and weaknesses in different arenas. The same foundation (you) is the thread throughout it all. Any practice involves failure and trying again, until you accomplish what you desire, and then you set another growth challenge and do it again. This process welcomes and relies on coaching and refining. In essence, practice is preparation for the game, performance, or competition. It's where the winning happens every day! I learned this sentiment from the words of Muhammad Ali.

Who you are in terms of your values and moral grounding—essentially, your character or foundation—automatically feeds into who you are as a leader. What motivates and challenges you as an individual channels itself directly into your leadership. A transformative leader is never idle. The work of drawing in the best of you and casting out the worst of you is constant and continuous.

Be content in your progress and successes but never in your learning. Let knowledge spark new innovation and new innovation spark knowledge. Then, lean into the wisdom that shows you how, when, and where to apply that knowledge effectively into your leadership journey. Your own development is purposed to foster growth in others. Give of what you have freely, and you will be given more.

The academic world was where I most consistently poured myself into leadership. I felt safe and supported in that realm because it offered many "take-charge" opportunities in structured environments, with clear expectations and defined success (i.e., grading system, honor roll, etc.). Still, there is always competition!

I recall very early on in grade school overhearing a discussion about whether or not I should be admitted to an advanced placement program as my older brother had been. But the teachers at that time believed that I was not as "gifted," mainly because I wasn't a reader (and still don't love it). That rejection fueled me and became a source of conviction to prove them wrong. And I did. The very next year, I made it in as an honor student right through college. Those honor cords worn on graduation day meant so much to me because I proved that what others say matters little but what you do matters very much. I was leading a life of achievement, proving to myself that I could go beyond expectations and doubts. Potential is limitless. When you acknowledge that, you become a living example of such.

However, leading and growth are not without their moments of challenge, failure, and downright ugliness. One such incident was in my early elementary years. I'll spare you the details, but suffice it to say there is a right and a wrong way to win, and I chose the latter. In a race where I was in the top two, I harnessed my innermost ugly and did what it took to win—I tripped the boy and sent him skidding to the ground. It's not a good look for a "leader," and it wasn't the kind of win I had intended. I couldn't enjoy my victory because I'd done it the wrong way. It's not a proud moment, but it is a teachable moment, and it stuck with me. Even at that young age, it impacted me for the better.

When you deeply want something, figure out a way to get it—*morally, ethically, and in a manner that upholds your values and your team.* You're commanding an outcome, and that makes you a leader. I'm not proud of how I seized this situation, but there are indeed valuable lessons to all moments in life. I felt ashamed of my behavior but gained character lessons that I've never forgotten—the most important at that moment being *how you win does matter.* This anonymous quote on the wall of a gym says it all: "Win with grace, lose with dignity." *Winning with grace* evidences humility and gratitude toward the opportunity and who got you there. It honors others. *Losing with dignity* understands that you have a purpose and value, just as others do. It's the ability to genuinely appreciate and celebrate the win of another. Both build character.

Leadership opportunities surround us every day, no matter who we are or what we do. Each opportunity offers a stronger sense of foundation and confidence. Today, I am less risk-averse. I navigate challenges well and have learned to adapt. My upbringing was the catalyst for problem-solving. It was likely the time I learned another crucial leadership skill: being the calm within the storm. In chaos, stressful situations, and tragedy, people look for guidance. Your own certainty and command of a situation will either draw in or repel others. Trust the discernment you've been given and what you've learned through every circumstance. Trust your purpose, and others will trust you.

The Evolving Leader

People often fear change, but the sometimes chaotic, shifting moments in life help us to evolve as leaders. We need to reshape that in our minds, too. "The only constant in life is change," as Heraclitus said. Change is normal; change is continual. Remaining the same without adapting, though sometimes quite comfortable and "safe"-feeling, is the exact opposite of where we should strive to be. One would certainly hope that my leadership looks very different now than my leadership in kindergarten or even than it did a year ago. Not entirely but in specific areas of growth. You evolve as you move through life, and the rules, the people, and the environments shift. They never remain the same, so how do you respond when the world isn't here to serve you what you expect? You simply and resiliently evolve.

In high school, I made decisions by simply sticking to what my teachers and parents had told me was the "right thing to do." College was a different environment. My moral compass was tested in a more diverse world, with many new sets of rules, magnified by the factor of many more people. I also was part of the Greek system, which brought its own experiences that would shape me into who I am today.

Sorority life was foreign to me, except pieces of the movie *Animal House* that friends told me about (I wasn't allowed to watch it). I doubted whether being in a sorority was the route I should take, but something recast my entire Greek experience. Most people remember Hurricane Andrew, but what they may not know is that weeks later, on September 11, 1992, Hurricane Iniki slammed into Kaua`i. I received that dreadful call from my mom on my way to class, a Category 4 hurricane on a direct path over our tiny island—the strongest hurricane recorded to have ever struck the Hawaiian islands. The dean of students made a difficult but necessary call to ensure the safety of the two of us who were from Kaua`i—we were to remain at school until further notice.

Days passed; news crews covered destruction to the outer islands but not from Kaua`i. One day, while I was out, one of my roommates received a call to relay that my family was alive (remember this is pre-cellular phone era). Later, I found out that our family's home was destroyed, along with much else on the island. It was devastating, as any natural disaster is. I communicated the update to my sorority at a chapter meeting and could not believe what happened next. These young college students who were just getting to know me emptied boxes of clothes and supplies from their closets and ran to the store for necessities. Their donations were placed into shipping containers and sent to Kaua`i. I was overwhelmed by their hearts of compassion and generosity—without being asked and without delay. I'll never forget the imprint that this outpouring of support left on me. My sorority sisters went out of their way to create a profound connection and make a lasting impact. They emulated what it looks like to be outward-facing, generous, and responsive.

I share my story to help you draw in specific times in your own life that shape who you are and the leader you are today. In each memory, recognize how *you've* evolved as a leader. Celebrate where you are right now in your career and in your leadership journey. The journey is a blessing because it allows us to learn in layers, without the need for perfection. There is something valuable on the other side of failure—another opportunity, a new day. Celebrate where you are now, and understand that with each new experience, you will adapt over time. This is a blessing. We can't learn everything all at once.

Life graciously places us with different people at different times and requires us to receive different equipping. Sometimes, I'll admit, it's exhausting to learn and be challenged constantly—but it's the path to elevating your potential beyond what you think you are capable of. No one really wants to leave their comfort zone, but for those who dare to pursue leadership as a gateway to impact and influence, it is essential. The leader you are now is a launching point for the leader you will most certainly become.

The Leader You Are

You influence the leader you are now and the leader you will become.

SPARKS OF TRUTH

- A leader becomes who they set out to be.
- A leader invests in their own personal and professional development.
- Leading is transformative for you and those you lead.
- Your leadership enables you to create a fountain of prosperity for yourself and those you lead.
- Character matters, always.

PROMPTS FOR IMPACT

- What is your leadership purpose and/or success statement in ten words or less?
- Write down the attributes that others express appreciation for in you.
- How are you investing in your own personal and professional growth?

NOTES

....

....

....

....

....

....

....

....

....

....

....

....

....

....

....

Humility isn't denying your strengths; it's being honest about your weaknesses.

—RICK WARREN

CHAPTER TWO

Confident Humility

confident: feeling or showing confidence in oneself; self-assured.

humility: freedom from pride or arrogance; holding a balanced opinion of oneself, especially in relation to others.

Harmony and balance are very good tools to apply in life. Using these concepts to evaluate and reset, or course-correct, is effective in continuous development. Separately, confidence and humility may seem to give you a picture of two opposing forces, but they actually complement each other. Pause with me to understand each separately.

Being confident lends to your own trust in your abilities and judgment. On one end is overconfidence—an inflated and false reality of self—and on the other end is being underconfident—having low appreciation for your abilities. Neither extreme bears healthy fruit. Turn now to humility, freedom from pride or arrogance, which lends to having an accurate opinion of yourself and your worth. A high opinion turns to pride, and a low one may diminish your worth and value as you become inwardly critical and outwardly envious. If you hold them in balance, confident humility is a natural tool to keep you from the extremes and sustain a place of productive balance.

Academics, sports, a job, and the like all are a training ground to learn the dark and light sides of failure and success, and of course, competition. Hula (Hawaiian dance) in my life presented a unique opportunity and challenge. As with anything, you work hard to learn and to master—the hours of commitment, sacrifice, and downright sweat give way to satisfaction, enjoyment, and more sweat. There is something about performing that is inspiring and deeply satisfying. When you look into the audience and see them smile, see them connect—you see them appreciate the experience you have the privilege of providing. It's a gift.

The other side of the good is always the danger zone. When you excel at something, you naturally gain confidence and recognition for your talent. The danger comes into play when you shift the focus off others and onto yourself. It opens the door that invites a prideful heart and an arrogant mind to settle in. The reason those traits are problem-stirrers is that they tend to leave the focus on you and create blind spots—an inflated ego that becomes a barrier to learning, hearing, and receiving and, ultimately, kills joy—the joy for both you and others.

Let someone else praise you, and not your mouth; an outsider, and not your own lips.

—Proverbs 27:2

Boasting of yourself is never received as well as the praise you get from someone else. The former is evidence of self-focus, and the latter is the fruit of focusing on others, on *serving* others. In college, I took on the opportunity to be one of the teachers for our school's annual lū'au. When it came time for staging, though I had the right as the instructor to place myself front and center on the stage, I placed myself in the second row—in a support position. There was a lot of talk about that decision! For me, it was simple. I looked at us as a team. It wasn't a solo; it was a group performance. I did what would look best and *be* best for the performance of that hula as a whole. I did what would hold the group in synergy and beautifully uniform movement to make it most impactful for the audience.

The integrity and quality of your leadership are shown when a benefit to *you* is expected, yet you flip it and use it to edify your team. When you focus on others above yourself, not aiming to gain a following or accolades but instead to surrender, you give others a chance to shine! I'm a believer that your best work isn't done in the limelight, but it's done behind the scenes. The gifts we receive and the hard work we put in are wasted if we aren't able to instruct and pour into others.

Confidence is oversold in our present times. A healthy place of confidence is by *knowing* who you are and believing in yourself. If you are trying to convince others, you're on the wrong track. In the absence of humility, confidence gives way to ego and arrogance, which spoils the fruit of your gifts. Humility is meant as an essential balance to confidence. It keeps you in a neutral space of learning and accepting rather than repelling and dismissing.

Confidence and humility together are powerful forces with a wealth of purpose. Humility alone is often viewed as an absence of strength. However, I see it and experience it as pureness and goodness, as selfless and open. It is something not common in our communities but clearly seen when it is present. It is the necessary complement to the building of a confident leader.

Humble Truth

Regardless of what generation you hail from, information is fed to you. As the technology age has ushered itself in at unprecedented speed and acceptance, it has brought with it a culture of instant gratification. When you don't know what something means, you can Google it. When you want something, you can order it at the click of a button. When you haven't seen someone, you can video call. In some ways, people aren't thinking for themselves, losing deductive reasoning and investigative learning. Information is fed and consumed differently than it has been before, and business or aspects of businesses are "innovating." This presents a new and exciting chance to reach people and expand our roles in ways that were not as critical previously. People, even in the age of technology, are still our greatest asset and privilege to safeguard as leaders.

You don't just *arrive* as a fantastic leader and manager one day. Holding this book right now, you realize that some things are missing from your toolkit and that acknowledgment will encourage you toward great leadership. You're allowing humility to show you ways to complement the leader you already are. Leading for Impact aims to broaden and deepen your perspective, skills, and stewardship over those you are responsible to lead, teach, and protect.

At a time when we're so freely given information, the importance of *truth* is greater than it ever has been. Truth is simple—true or false, core issue, root cause. Moving in blind trust to believe and follow any human is dangerous and counter to your own understanding and learning. Now more than ever, it's important to consider where information comes from. Truth is that deductive reasoning—taking the time to dive into sources, reasoning, and logical flow.

Questioning is so important because it causes you to glean assurance to build on what you believe. There are uncompromising standards in mathematics, science, statistics, peer reviews, and independent audits that establish and safeguard a society that is stable and prosperous. Questioning your own ideals, ideas, and actions is a humble step toward challenging and testing your own foundation. *Humility is essential to welcome truth and to allow yourself to be teachable.*

Discovering the truth through your morals/values/ethics base allows steadiness in everything that you do. Faith and value-led truth is my North Star. It builds my foundation and leads to discernment. Truth is centering. Be wise in how and where you acquire that truth and then even wiser in how you apply that truth. The never-ending journey! Having the humility to seek your truth and a *broader* truth is the epitome of leading for impact.

Humility through Vulnerability

At its core, humility shows *vulnerability*, which is a word some may not be comfortable with within the traditional, professional scope. I was certainly one who initially dismissed this word and what it implied. My CEO group holds me accountable. Working with them led me to realize that vulnerability enables you and others to get to know the roots of who you are. It's a requirement. Being vulnerable is difficult but necessary for becoming a credible *connection point* for others, especially staff members. I see it all the time—when others recognize that you've stumbled or experienced failure, it gives them a bit of relief. Showcasing the humanness in you creates stronger connections and trust.

My husband and I were discussing ministry. I'm a believer, and he is not (or dare I say, *not yet*), and he jokingly shared the sentiment, "Oh, you think you're perfect?" It was a great moment because I got to share my self-perception with him. "The fact of the matter is that I, in full view of myself, see quite the opposite. I see how *very imperfect* I am. I see all of my flaws and failures, and yet I'm still incredibly loved." That is truth—reality without self-destruction.

This moment stays with me, reminding me of my gratitude. Love, despite my human moments, is what makes me secure. Who wouldn't embrace that? Yes, I can fall on my face, but for me, I know nothing and no one in all creation can snatch me from the hand of God. As far as my own "shortcomings" (sin is too heavy a truth for many, but really the only accurate way to relate the gravity of the *me* that exists if left to my own selfish ambition, self-promotion, and/or self-preservation)—the *me* that likes to go my own way, I am a work in process, devoted to excellence, and short of perfection.

I am grateful that by God's own mercy and grace, it is not up to me. His gifts, equipping, and good purpose are what give me value. What my husband saw was my confidence and strength. It was profound to share with him that it was the actual outworking of, yes, my faith but also my imperfection. I know that I stumble and fall every day. I have flaws. I know I've got a lot to work on, and yet I have the security of my moral foundation, faith, and the love of my family. These gifts humble me every day and provide confidence and security.

I bring all this up to highlight how security and confidence really come from the selflessness that allows true connection to others. Without humility, there is no authenticity—it's a mask, a wall of false pretenses, and you can't break through it. Those with large egos can't deeply listen. Have you encountered leaders who don't feel present with you? Inauthentic? On social media, I saw a post quoting Elon Musk. It said, "Please note that Twitter will do lots of dumb things in the coming months. We will keep what works and change what doesn't." I don't know much about him, but like most of you, I'm familiar with Tesla and SpaceX. I thought to myself, "Wow, here's someone who is ushering in remarkable innovation, a billionaire, and he is telling the whole world that he would make mistakes."

There's power (even awe) in humility. There's power in vulnerability and telling others that you might mess up. Everyone will see it. There will be bad days and you'll be grumpy, disenchanted, frustrated—you name it. Everyone will see it all. At the end of the day, that's just you being human, but it's what you *do* in your full humanity that counts. Action always reigns king. I like the doers who live what they believe. There's tremendous humility in a leader rolling up their sleeves and getting into the mix—not sitting behind closed doors and giving directives but truly and earnestly standing beside their teams in collaboration and in honest truth. *That's authentic strength. Deep, meaningful leadership reaches your inner self and touches lives.*

Confident Imperfection

Profound tragedy has hit members of our team on more than one occasion, as is the story of life lived by people. Humility and vulnerability allow us to see the *person* in these circumstances. As is our pattern to come alongside and support our employees, I once told someone to take as much time as they needed. I asked how we could all support them and their family through this tough time. Here was one response: "Jennifer, this is my sanctuary. This is where I come for normalcy. This is where I come to just feel secure and stable." When you receive a response like this, it makes the pursuit of confident humility so worth it, and not only that, it makes it imperative.

A former contract employee expressed that he'd never seen a group where the values were so evident. It flows from the managers and leaders into the whole company and comes out through the contractors. Comments like this reiterate why strong-rooted leadership is so crucial. The work you're doing as you pour into others will, in turn, inspire others to do the same. Grounding yourself in humility will offer an abundance of confidence and then instill this same confidence in others. They feel valued, they feel seen and heard, and they have firm ground beneath their feet.

There's a good chance that humility is not how anyone arrives at a leadership position, but the process of being given leadership opportunities demands humility—a necessary component of authentic confidence. I'm not the CEO because I'm an incredible person who landed on a natural trajectory. I'm here because I have a purpose, and I'm here because of all the various people who surrounded me at different stages of my life, whom I'm grateful for. My current team and the teams of the past and the future are essential to my leadership journey.

Taking a deep inventory of one's self is important to determining how you see yourself in relation to others, who you're serving, and what you hold as valuable. The hula story at the beginning of this chapter set the stage (pardon the pun) for this ability in me. I was a teacher, serving both my students and our audience. My purpose was to develop an enchanting performance to entertain our audience. Embracing humility allowed me to channel my talent toward my students and foster a beautiful production for the joy of our audience, above any other self-serving purpose or outcome. I'm committed to both my strengths and my imperfections. Your leadership journey has the same core. You have gifts to nurture others, to serve others, and to impact others.

Confident Character

To "stay the course" in difficult times, you have to believe in doing the right thing, all the time. The confidence factor came deeper into focus for me in 2020. Everything was shutting down due to COVID-19, as you're well aware. Business leaders had to navigate unprecedented hardships that had "life or death" potential and also the potential to cripple and destroy a business—the livelihoods of people. Summit Group is first and foremost focused on people, and we maintained this stance over the dollar, during a time when there was the potential to experience enormous financial loss. We chose and managed to preserve the company with one priority in mind. We held onto *something bigger*—people. Confidence arises from moral conviction.

Fear decays truth and is a weapon for destruction. It was the single-most common trait I witnessed during 2020 and 2021. As we reached out to the community to work together to preserve jobs, as best we could, it was eye-opening to see who came to the table and who slammed the doors. Fear breeds self-preservation. We weren't able to save every position, but we did advocate strongly. We are a small business that hurt a lot with our community, but we did what we could to care for our team and give back, even during a time of want instead of plenty. We didn't allow the circumstances to stop us or diminish our impact. Our system of values was unbeaten by what happened in the world. It was always there. We were confident in our convictions and still are.

Our world is changing rapidly and will continue to do so. It is *simple.* Not easy, but simple. No matter what's happening, I'll stick to what I know and deeply believe to be true. I won't let factors or people shake the immovable foundation given to me. The COVID-19 experience changed so much around us and shook people to their core, even from their own foundations. There were so many unknowns, and everyone sought some shred of stability—they looked to leaders to provide courage and strength.

Prioritizing others anchored me, as well as my unshakeable faith. In the end, calm devotion to others will guide you through any situation. Today, we still are navigating the effects of decisions made for us and our communities; the market has shifted, the economy is threatened, and the world stage is different. Tomorrow will bring a new challenge or uncertainty and, with it, new ways to show the strength of your leadership character. Character always matters. You were made for such a time as this.

Confident Humility

CHAPTER SPOTLIGHT

Humility fosters an accurate and genuine reflection of yourself, your shortcomings, and worth.

SPARKS OF TRUTH

- Humility will show you ways to complement the leader you already are.

- Humility is essential to welcome truth and learning.

- Humility doesn't shy away from weaknesses and imperfections.

- Fear decays truth and is a weapon for destruction.

PROMPTS FOR IMPACT

- Self-inventory: Where are you overconfident and/or under-confident in leadership?

- What is your greatest fear as a leader?

- How will you create a safe space to fail forward?

NOTES

....

....

....

....

....

....

....

....

....

....

....

....

....

....

....

Leadership and learning
are indispensable
to each other.

—JOHN F. KENNEDY

CHAPTER THREE

Servant Warrior

servant: one that serves others; to be worthy of reliance or trust.

warrior: a brave or experienced soldier or fighter.

Think of the warrior leader—the legend of strength, certainty, and power. There's almost a militaristic aspect to the word. *Warrior* means fortitude, order, and authority. When it comes to the *servant*, it's associated with someone being humble, sacrificial, helpful, but lacking in authority. There's no contradiction between these two words from where I stand. The servant warrior is a leader to follow. If you are one or the other, good on you! Your natural strengths are likely in one camp. This is a challenge to bring them together and see where it takes your leadership reflection.

In our current world, there is such a strong desire for a sense of identity and acceptance. People seem uncertain of who they are and what their purpose is in life. Identities are placed on shifting sand, in the hands of others, and on false premises. That's why it's unstable and scary! For a long time, my identity was about doing well in school, and then it transitioned to excelling at work. *I work hard, I succeed, and I reach new heights.* That was what gave me purpose. I realized that these qualities weren't who I am; they were what I *do*. I am my values: honesty, reliability, diligence, and so on. In this chapter, we'll discuss how I embraced the servant aspect within my natural warrior.

Servant's Battle

Most of us have a big, beautiful river between ourselves and others—*us and them*. The servant sees another story outside of their own, based on the reality of difference—what the other was born into, what experiences they had, and what their values are. There's dignity in looking at another and witnessing similarities and differences while fully appreciating the other person.

The servant leader invites respect and honors differences. They're interested in learning someone else's story, not just playing out their own. In recruiting, this interest in others is essential. When someone walks through the door, it's not about me but instead being interested in them. What's their story, and where do they intersect with our values? Sadly, there are too few servants who are willing to invite people to the table, build a bridge, or even lend their bridge to someone who can't build their own.

I love the concept of *gathering*. In Hawai'i, that's what we do. We gather to eat, to "talk story," to sing, to dance; we just come together! It's amazing to see people come and share a table. We often don't have individual seats. We sit together on a bench and contend with the fact that we are all sandwiched between other people, sometimes strangers. It's a launching point to *interaction* between people. It is a compulsory connection that works; it just does. As humans, we were made to share all our senses, to engage, and to deepen the bonds among one another.

I bring up this Hawaiian tradition because it highlights humility and the sacrificial heart that looks at others through the genuine lens of *I want to know more about you*. On a leadership level, I want you to reach your full potential, so how can I help you do that? I know many leaders—including myself in earlier versions—who have a "follow me" approach. They're headed somewhere no matter what, and they instruct others to follow in their wake. This is the warrior, but the servant turns to those behind them and offers to walk alongside them.

I noticed this in ministry. You might desire to see an area of growth in someone, a stronghold defeated, or get them to recognize something life-changing, but they may not be ready. If they're not ready, it's not your job to rule their life. In ministry, it *was* our job to see, lead, and be of service to the person sacrificially and with a heart to foster transformation. The servant leader comes alongside in this same way, while the warrior wants to lead and forge the path. There's nothing wrong with that. We need warriors in leadership roles, but it is the servant warrior who forges the path while having the ability to adapt, learn, and invite others along for the journey. The combination of these skills is critical.

Many are successful at the warrior style, but the challenge is that this approach is not the deep, authentic leader we're capable of being. The servant without the warrior is just a servant. The warrior without the servant is just a warrior. The combination is a leader of influence and transformation. You need the drive and passion, the vision of excellence, but you also require compassion and authenticity to be a catalyst to bring major goals to fruition.

Some crave the warrior type of leader whose strengths tend to be setting expectations and actions. There are others who see the warrior and retreat or run in the opposite direction in fear or lack of readiness, even desire. Particularly in today's climate. Conversely, if you are a servant warrior who can walk beside others, listen, lift up—put yourself aside sacrificially—then it's clear that the mission you're on is that of and for the people. If I might flip the idea on its head, in my mind, the latter is the definition of a true warrior. One who both leads and lifts, not for their own victories, but for the raising up of others in those wins.

Illuminating the servant warrior isn't possible without a discussion of competitiveness—rampant when we're growing up and also as adults. Some people don't grow out of it. For me, friendship has always been worth more than any position or accomplishment (maybe the servant was there all along?). For some, their position is all they have right now for crafting their identity, well-being, or sense of safety—at any stage in life. I'm sure you know this type of person. Many of them are leaders, but the kind you don't want to follow, let alone walk beside. *Upholding and valuing other people is a relational path to success.*

It took many years for the servant aspect of leadership to take root in me. It was leadership in ministry that shaped me into the servant leader I was purposed to be. I was called upon to teach children. Looking into the eyes of kids, somehow they know whether or not you're telling the truth, when you are nervous, and when you genuinely care for them. They are intuitive and trusting, and my time spent teaching them was a high calling (that I didn't ask for!). At the time, I thought to myself, "You must have the wrong Jennifer," because teaching children didn't seem to align with who I thought I was, but there was a need, and I have always sought to fill any void that existed.

Perhaps you already have the warrior spirit within, but the servant piece is coming more slowly, as it did for me. It takes many experiences before you can see it—before humility melds with the take-charge general within. You might notice that experiences are placing you where you are *needed* and not where you want to be. You're stretched outside your comfort zone. In my case, there I was, accountable to the youth, and currently, accountable to my (obviously) grown team. Being a parent will teach you this on a whole different level, too. The servant in me was born out of necessity. I was called upon by other people, called for a purpose, and it transformed my perspective on life. Accepting any position to lead with the intention of giving of yourself to raise up the best in others is the heart and soul of the servant warrior.

All of this makes me think of the allegorical poem, "Footprints in the Sand." A man looks back at his life through the lens of footprints—his own and the Lord's. He notices times where one set of footprints disappears. In natural leaps to assumptions, this poem presents a picture of transformational perspective:

FOOTPRINTS IN THE SAND

One night a man had a dream. He dreamed

he was walking along the beach with the LORD.

Across the sky flashed scenes from his life.

For each scene he noticed two sets of

footprints in the sand: one belonging

to him, and the other to the LORD.

When the last scene of his life flashed before him,

he looked back at the footprints in the sand.

He noticed that many times along the path of

his life there was only one set of footprints.

He also noticed that it happened at the very

lowest and saddest times in his life.

This really bothered him and he

questioned the LORD about it:

"LORD, you said that once I decided to follow

you, you'd walk with me all the way.

But I have noticed that during the most

troublesome times in my life,

there is only one set of footprints. I don't understand why when

I needed you most you would leave me."

The LORD replied:

"My son, my precious child,

I love you and I would never leave you.

During your times of trial and suffering,

when you see only one set of footprints,

it was then that I carried you."

The servant warrior goes into battle for others. There's nothing quite like seeing the fruits of your labor when others flourish. The warrior alone can't look from left to right and relish in others' triumphs, but the servant warrior has a broader awareness of being—appreciating where each person is going along the journey. Remember, the warrior looks forward. *What's coming? What are the challenges?* They're forging a path, while the servant is interested in the flow. The process, if you will. *How can I serve this person? How can I get this person from point A to point B? Who do I need to ask for help?* That last question is so important. Many leaders think they have to do it on their own. It's OK to ask for help, it's humbling, and it's a great way to lead by example.

I do not intend to judge any leadership style. If you're a warrior, then be what you are, the best version of it! But if you're a servant warrior, you actively bring more people along for the journey. You raise them up to be servant warriors themselves. They're not just following. You're inviting people along the way. Where the warrior is going headfirst, the servant has the full awareness of who's falling behind, brings them up, and helps them to their destination.

A word that I love to call upon is *discernment.* The warrior says, "I know the destination. Keep up!" But the servant warrior exhibits discernment and understanding when people might not want to reach the destination you are directing them toward. They may not comprehend the benefit or opportunities being presented, and you have to use a discerning mind and approach to get them to discover the benefit for themselves.

When leading for impact, you can forge a path while also helping people up when they fall. You can lead the way while also inviting others to walk beside you. You're not just reaching a destination, but you're also guiding with your whole self, helping others to arrive at their fullest potential—releasing dollars, time, and energy in the process. None of this is a waste. You're *enriching* your integrity, reputation, and, ultimately, the lives of others.

You step aside at times to allow others the opportunity to showcase their own ways to lead, and you support them as they do so. You encourage them into and *allow* for them to have their moment. That's authentic power. If you don't have this pause button inside of you, arrogance can easily take over—contrary to humility. Choosing the servant warrior approach does require more time, effort, and *introspection*. It's sacrificial, and it's transformational, for you and for those you lead.

Introspective Servant

So much of the servant aspect is responding to a purpose and a calling while also realizing that you're human. Be willing to accept yourself with the intent of reaching your best. You can know yourself (the leader you are) while also accepting your flaws. Case in point: I was checking in at the airport when the attendant greeted my son and me, asking, "How was your day?" Before I could say anything, my son looked up at her and shared, "My mom said a bad word in the car." I did and admitted to the offense. She humorously replied, "Well, I would've believed him anyway whether you admitted it or not." A leader owns up to their mistakes.

In my case, they are too numerous to count, and I admit it freely. My life actions admit it for me! Acknowledging and accepting yourself is helpful when leading others who are *also* human and doing their best. Without this introspection and acceptance, leadership isn't authentic, and the truth will be known regardless of whether you own up to it or not. Truth is truth, and it has its natural way of showing up when you least expect it.

As you know from chapter 1, my leadership now looks different from how it used to. That's not to say that I lost the warrior, but today I understand when the warrior needs to take the lead and—oftentimes—when it doesn't. That infuses in me a healthier, more purposeful balance. Believe it or not, you can be more productive and fruitful when you're mindful about the warrior, intentional about the servant, and not just immediately *reacting*. You can step back, view, assess, and *respond*. You can value the warrior while nurturing the servant each day.

In my formative years, this bossy bit of goods had a fight in her. I recall going out to eat with my friends, and if we got bad service at the table, the anticipation was palpable. *Oh my goodness, here it comes*, they thought. My friends knew that I wouldn't stand for it! I was polite as well as fierce. This tenacity reared its head in both directions. If someone was unkind to another, out of the blue and for no good reason, I was the first person to stand next to the one who was wronged and stand up to the offender. Essentially, my warrior spirit was alive and well, but I hadn't harbored the servant. My leadership role provided a huge breakthrough. *If I'm the person who always takes the lead, who always jumps in, then I'm preventing someone else from having the opportunity to be the one to step forward. I'm hindering their ability to grow.*

It's important to discuss restraint in service. Do the themes of *withholding* and *servanthood* seem weak? If so, it's only because society has taught us that. In truth, these are tremendous strengths. This reminds me of a story to recount from my son's preschool years. My daughter was in Taekwondo at the time, and we'd travel to the dojo to watch for a few hours while she practiced. Our family was dedicated to her training. Leaving the parking lot, an Amber Alert came on the radio—an emergency announcement informing community members of a child abduction. I kept my focus on driving, not allowing anything to divert my attention. The announcement didn't hit me until my son asked, "Mom, is that for real?"

I kept my mind steady, trying to get out of the chaotic parking lot, "Is what for real?" I responded. He gently asked, "What they said on the radio?" Something in the back of my mind had registered the message. "Yes, buddy. It is." He immediately said, "We should pray." The parking lot was hairy, to say the least, and even though my goal was to get out of there, I pulled into a vacant spot and turned to my son. "You're right, buddy. Yeah, we should pray."

I had an agenda for that day, and my brain had been going in a million directions, but praying for that tragic incident seemed spot-on. A mother had lost a child. My son knew it and was the first to pray. The twist to this story has forever changed my perspective. You see, my first thought was for the safety of the child and the grief of the mom—because that is what I related to, but it was on my son's heart to pray for the "bad man whose heart didn't know Jesus." I sat there witnessing the honesty of a child seeing the brokenness of others. He did not reproach or condemn, but asked, "Why did that man do it? Why is he so broken?"

As I stood in front of an audience recounting this story, I paused, humbled by the memory of my son's moment—his servant heart, folded within the servant warrior who wished to pray. All eyes on me, I was supposed to be the authority, the teacher. I felt privileged to be in that position and also to be humbled and learn from a child. I am far from a perfect example. I am just like everybody else. I stumble. I see what I did and didn't do. Here I am, owning up to the fact that a brave, innocent child taught me what to do.

I not only share my faith with you but also hold space in this journey for you as a person, regardless of what your own beliefs may be. They fit into your story and your leadership right now. We're all here in our full humanity. We stumble and we fall. We don't do the right things at certain points in time. Own up to and acknowledge your mistakes. You're still *you* while learning much along the way. On top of that, there's a very good chance that you picked up this book with the warrior already pounding its drum inside of you, and you've come to a place in life where you're seeking the servant. Welcome. There's so much more to explore!

Servant Warrior

CHAPTER SPOTLIGHT

The servant warrior is trustworthy to persevere through challenges and uphold the dignity of others.

SPARKS OF TRUTH

- The servant leader invites respect and honors differences.
- The servant warrior gives of themselves to raise up others.
- A servant leader fosters a relational path to success.
- A servant warrior is not afraid to be a student.

PROMPTS FOR IMPACT

- Share a time when someone carried you and a time when you carried another.
- Where do you need to be a better student? How will you do it?
- How will you actively emulate a servant warrior leadership style?

NOTES

....
....
....
....
....
....
....
....
....
....
....
....
....
....

In a world of algorithms, hashtags, and followers, know the true importance of human connection.

—UNKNOWN

CHAPTER FOUR

Relational Relevance

relational: the way in which two or more people or things are connected.

relevance: the quality or state of being closely connected; when something is "relevant," it means it matters.

Relational relevance refers to the *people* component of business. In spite of advances in technology, remote work flexibility, and so on, we are relational beings; nothing can substitute fully for another human being—as much as I love animals, especially dogs, not even them. Even the most introverted person has a natural longing for connection with others. This highlights the importance of being rooted in who you are, as a person and a leader.

Living your values enables you to treat others with respect and create a meaningful connection. Finding common ground with others, in spite of your differences, is an essential life and leadership skill. This is also where the humility side of confidence and the servant side of the warrior play an important role. Accepting yourself and being aware of your own faults will set you in a healthy place to accept others for their strengths *and* their shortcomings—to look outward and help others achieve more.

There is no time more pressing than the present for our companies to go beyond our traditional roles to develop our teams and future leaders, deepen our connections, and celebrate the *people* behind the initiatives and goals. Summit Group Solutions is invested in people—dedicated to being that positive influence in our field. Our foundation is *a foundation of people*—not of staffing, business, or revenue but of people.

People matter most, and we are seeing the raw exposure of this truth in our current culture. Companies are seeking a balanced approach to core business purposes and awareness of unique team needs. A prosperous business can press forward and care over their people, too. Leaders are the catalysts who can forge this productive path forward. Creating strong connections with others requires a strong awareness of yourself. Understanding yourself and investing in your own personal and professional development are critical to fostering strong relationships that endure. The desire to help others in the smallest of ways and the eagerness to see and celebrate their successes are the markers of servant leadership, and that journey begins with *you*.

Creating a connection involves taking your eyes off yourself and being genuinely interested in others, in their stories. The core values we commit to as a team have been what cultivates that genuine interest in others and unifies us in a common purpose. Our teams of the past, present, and certainly those still to come represent a beautifully unique group of people, different in personality, approach, communication, interests, and so on but committed to the same core values. Everyone comes to the table with their individual worth, but collectively, we agree on company pillars to abide by, uniting who we are as a whole. Absent this unifying force, differences and self-elevation breed disconnection and difficulties that could potentially destroy that internal culture—which is the staying power and heartbeat of the company.

Our team uses the acronym DIDAI to remember our values: dignity, integrity, diligence, achievement, and impact. It is our work-family story. Each person is welcomed with the dignity intended for them and embraced for the personal imprint they make on the team and the business operations. We expect everyone to operate with integrity—humble fortitude—doing what's right every day, especially when it's hard or unpopular.

It's important to establish a pattern so that in those times that you stumble (and we all will), you don't destroy your reputation because it's so much harder to uphold your reputation than to destroy it. Every day we expect each member of our team to be results oriented and be relied upon to work hard: diligence. Together, as a team, we celebrate our achievements (the outworking of dignity, integrity, and diligence) with enthusiasm and gratitude. For us, our story, or end goal (vision), culminates in impact. We strive to build strong relationships in business and in our communities where we live and work. Each person brings their individual gifts and talents, and commits to using them to serve others generously.

DIGNITY

- We *value* the worth of every person.

- We are *committed* to honoring each other with kindness and respect.

INTEGRITY

- We *value* humble fortitude.

- We are *committed* to living out strong moral principles to uphold our reputation.

DILIGENCE

- We *value* results.

- We are *committed* to daily perseverance, reliability, and hard work.

ACHIEVEMENT

- We *value* winning as a team.

- We are *committed* to celebrating our accomplishments with enthusiasm and gratitude.

IMPACT

- We *value* positive relationships in business and in the community.

- We are *committed* to using our individual gifts and talents to serve others generously.

In essence, DIDAI sets our sights on what matters most—people, *relational relevance.* It starts with dignity. When we welcome someone, we value and respect them for who they are and what they're bringing to the table. The other bookend is *impact.* Everything we do for the candidates, clients, company, and community represents the impact we strive for every day. That's our vision in action (not what you have but what you have to give). It's relational relevance enriched to serve a positive purpose.

Leadership Commitment

Defining values and upholding them require commitment and authority. Though *order* and *authority* (similar to *servanthood*) may not be appealing words in today's climate, they *do* have an important role in business. The current culture works to make irrelevant any word or thought that doesn't "fit" a particular ideal or liking. New knowledge is conjured up and sold by creating new jargon to redefine "outdated" terms, sometimes even to redefine reality. However, wisdom applied to knowledge allows one to see past personal preferences and alternate perspectives, realizing the value of certain things that may even make us uncomfortable.

Relationally relevant order and authority actually put people first—before dollars, goals, initiatives, and so on. It establishes bumpers that aid in keeping people focused together, despite differences. It recognizes and appreciates authority (don't discount the warrior), which creates security and stability, and establishes known expectations. This all works in unified force to cause people, individually and collectively, to thrive and reach new heights.

Order provides guideposts—it points to light, so none needlessly walk in darkness. A lawful society is established with order and authority to perpetuate safety, unity, and agreement on foundational principles of right and wrong. A deeper perspective into "authority" proves the usefulness of establishing order and guidelines. Leadership strategies and standards influence thoughts, development, and actions of people groups. At the end of the day, people follow certain leaders for varying reasons.

Innovative leaders adapt their strategies and approaches to meet the needs of those they have authority over. They are responsive rather than reactive or exclusive. Some adapt well, and some do not. Influential leaders lean into relational relevance, especially in our post-Gen X, post-COVID-19 age that has ushered in new challenges. Rolex watches, retirement savings, and *loyalty* have been transcended by new indulgent rewards: "unlimited" PTO (paid time off), remote work, etc. Leaders of today must understand, educate, and adapt, but they must also be intentional to cultivate and preserve a culture that fosters prosperity. Demands on both sides have to reasonably find common ground without losing productivity—being mindful of employer risks and costs, along with employee goals and desires.

Accountability is enfolded in order and authority, too—another word that separates top performers and leaders. When I'm working with my team and something goes wrong, or a mistake is made, I need to know who's accountable. Without accountability, everyone shares in the mistake, and professional development takes a back seat. The new way of leading for some is to lead with emotion, not wanting to make anyone uncomfortable. There is a false assumption of security in not bearing responsibility. Growth is uncomfortable, and uncomfortable is actually normal.

If everyone gets a trophy and no one stands out, who gets promoted? How do problems get solved, and when does the learning happen? If no one is held accountable, vital lessons are lost, and the path forward becomes unclear. Without someone in charge, there are too many cooks in the kitchen. Yes, collaboration is wonderful, but even in collaboration, someone must be facilitating and moving things forward. Otherwise, we are left to our own undeveloped talents, paces, and self-preservation instincts that work against raising the bar for ourselves and others.

I love the term *balancing the bully*. You don't have to be a bully to be a boss. We evolve as leaders throughout our journeys. We learn as we go, and continuous personal and professional growth is crucial. There's a learning curve, and fully embracing accountability will enhance your growth. When you fix problems or create solutions, you learn from failures along the way. Leaders have the opportunity to create an environment that rewards growth and removes fear from failure. Don't shy away from being the boss. Show authority and strength (as a servant warrior), and there will be no need to concern yourself with the traits of a bully. A bully is the opposite of strength; it belongs to one who is filled with fear and insecurity and lacks skill, compassion, and wisdom to walk in the shoes of a leader. Rise to the occasion, remove the bully, and be the example to follow.

Order and authority embrace the system of learning and teaching, even sacrifices, to enable others to shine. There are many times that it may be easier and faster to just tell others what to do so that something gets done, and you can move on. Indeed, it takes more time to invest in that relational component—to sit beside someone and teach them, show them, and let them do; to understand and observe their styles, barriers, and obstacles. It's important to ask questions and encourage questions. Use phrasing like "tell me ____," and "share why ____" so that you establish freedom to receive and hear the strengths and areas ripe for development from those you lead. Invest in them, in that relational space, so that you are better equipped to understand where that other person is coming from. You're seeking to understand how they think so that you can come alongside them and nurture their development.

So many leaders talk *at* people (you probably know a few). It does work sometimes for some people, and it's rather simple and efficient for whoever is directing in that manner, but it's also low in relational investment. People may do what you say, but are you fostering a dependency and stunting valuable growth and ownership? Leading by coming alongside people in this way will cost you, but your investment in them is a relational element that may be priceless, and the development that ensues is fruitful for the individual and the company, and even for the leader. Leaders develop themselves as they teach, coach, and mentor others. They create a solid foundation by investing in people. Relational relevance through your leadership commitment builds a strong team foundation.

Emotional Wellness

Leadership is enhanced by relational relevance. For us, it's always been important, but COVID-19 magnified its need and absence in places. Millennials came in with a whole new perspective that helped to reshape our professional landscape—challenging old ways and providing us with new opportunities while advancing innovation. This shift was not only generational but also ushered in a different culture in whole. This was magnified in 2020–2021, especially, as some responses to COVID-19 caused incredible isolation and loss of in-person touch points.

A new norm created itself: some marked exciting, welcome shifts, and some reactive, potentially harmful, new habits and entitlements. The most impactful losses I am witnessing stem from that lack of human connection. I would argue that the people factor is vital when leading for impact. It can't all be done online or remote, regardless of the new ways technology aims to bridge the connection gap; nothing substitutes standing beside or sitting with another human.

Technology and social media have also played a role in highlighting why the people factor is so fundamental. You'll recall the days when you did wrong in school, and it was just your friend beside you saying, "Oh, that's so embarrassing!" Perhaps there was some gossip surrounding what you did wrong. Now, if you mess up on social media, it feels like the whole world knows and people don't hold back their opinions. They lay into you, and that's hard on the psyche.

Technology has ushered in a place for cowards to prey and integrity to be cast aside. Never before has there been a greater invitation for people to say (or type) things that they wouldn't say face-to-face (which to me has always been the mark of a coward). Many don't even use their real names or pictures of themselves. This trend is so dangerous for one's integrity and accountability. People are putting their confidence, self-respect, self-affirmation, and self-*everything* in what is said about them, or whether they get a *thumbs-up*, *like*, *follow*, or *subscribe*.

We went from "words will never harm me" to words from absolute strangers and even bots making or breaking someone's day. Put the phones away, leave your laptop, and go grab a human and play a sport, grab some food, or enjoy a walk. Look people in the eye and talk to them. There's accountability when standing in front of someone and having to filter or reshape your thoughts for the sake of dialogue and reconciliation. Face-to-face human etiquette leads to healthy growth and personal development. Take it all in; that relational filling is relevant to each of us. It matters and is critical to our whole being.

I would name the new Goliath to be technology, the growing leaders are David, and the stone we must defend ourselves with is relational relevance, in a necessary movement to protect emotional wellness. I'm not a big social media person and don't like to post that often. My husband tells me, regarding Twitter and Instagram, that you have to be *all in*. Either you do it or you don't. You can't dabble. It most certainly can suck the "life" out of you—time, energy, brain power, emotion, and so on.

Even the purest remarks can be twisted into a dagger. There is simply no winning yet many losses. It's a game of diminishing returns. It adds so much hypocrisy to the movement of "inclusion." The online social media world is quick to pass judgment, dismiss intention, and proliferate labels and stereotypes. It resorts to name-calling, amplifies groupthink over individual reasoning, and offers no reconciliation and no accountability. It's a space ripe for destruction, if left to the uncoached and left with an empty portion of relational relevance. The interest in another and their unique stories are showered over by quick, and often false, assumptions. *People are divided, and emotional wellness seems more concerning than ever before. Society keeps getting further from relational relevance.*

This relational relevance, the stone for the new Goliath of technology, is a tool and not a weapon for leaders of today and of the future. We must protect ourselves from divisive negativity and consciously embrace the importance of human connection. If leaders don't take on this giant, technology will continue to be the bully on the field. As leaders, we need to hold ourselves more accountable than ever in this climate of depression, anxiety, and disease.

Protecting emotional wellness is now an all-powerful necessity for modern leaders. Some were isolated and masked for so long, and do you recall how grumpy everyone became—the fear, the stagnant skills, and the tragic losses? If you're not intentionally meeting the needs of others through investment, commitment, and hard work, then the house of cards will crumble. Everything you hope to accomplish will fall apart. People are more aware of this than ever before. Old leadership styles stripped away this crucial call for well-being. We're currently trying to recapture it (maybe even revolutionize it!) and hold it with care. *Leadership adaptation and transformation are not a choice. It's a key to the future of your business and your teams.*

When we lose sight of relational relevance, we lose sight of the inherent value of a person. People aren't *people* anymore. They become easily distanced objects. We dehumanize when we make others flat and treat them like *things*, dismissing their dignity and importance. Leading for impact means investing and committing our attention to connection. If we, as leaders, lack this commitment, then we collectively give up the battle. As we stare at the new Goliath, remember the people you lead. We're all purposed for something. See it in others. Develop it in yourself and *foster that purpose in others*. Relational relevance seeks to leave no one behind.

Relational Relevance

Relational relevance makes people "top of mind."

SPARKS OF TRUTH

- Relational relevance refers to the *people* component of business.

- Accepting yourself and being aware of your own shortcomings set you in a healthy place to accept others.

- Order and authority embrace the system of learning and teaching.

- Accountability fosters ownership development and creates a leadership-driven environment.

- Employee wellness is a growing concern among leadership.

PROMPTS FOR IMPACT

- What values establish your work culture?

- How will you cultivate relational relevance in your teams?

- Whom do you need to invest in right now? How?

- What measures will you take to foster emotional wellness for you and your team?

NOTES

....

....

....

....

....

....

....

....

....

....

....

....

....

....

Sacrifice is a part of life. It's supposed to be. It's not something to regret. It's something to aspire to.

—MITCH ALBOM

CHAPTER FIVE

Leading Sacrificially

sacrifice: the act of giving up (surrendering) something that is valuable to you in order to help someone else.

Intentional, impactful leadership requires you to look at the leader you are and the leader you wish to become. Now, turn the leadership lens outward toward sacrificial leadership. This process is intended to deflate the ego a bit because we're using a word that is contrary to strength and power in business and in our culture today: *sacrifice*. In this chapter, we'll bring the true meaning of sacrifice to light and explore or discover your initial attitude toward it, as well as how you might live it out in your own leadership.

Being a sacrificial leader goes beyond servant leadership. It encompasses the most humble lens of all. Where servant leadership involves an organizational ecosystem, being sacrificial goes a level deeper. It involves serving others through sacrificial means. *Leading sacrificially means setting boundaries, enforcing consequences, and sometimes not being well liked in difficult moments of decision.* It is truly doing what is best for the person regardless of whether that is what they want and possibly even what they don't want.

Sacrificial leading sets your own desires aside and focuses on upholding others. It also means letting go. Parenting has taught me how to lead sacrificially. When you're a parent, you have to set boundaries and be willing to execute the consequences with the intention of serving your children well—lifting them, supporting them. You shouldn't issue idle threats. If you say it, you have to commit to it. For me, that means that I have to be willing to sacrifice, too. This brings a story to mind.

When my daughter was just shy of her fifth birthday, she had a spell of the "naughties." We were getting ready to meet some friends at a beach barbecue. Unfortunately, her behavior became disrespectful, and I decided to issue the warning, "If you don't listen and behave then we're not going to the party." She matched my conviction with stubborn intensity and rose to the challenge. It was another teachable moment. We didn't make it to the BBQ, but we talked about how the impact of our actions and decisions goes beyond just ourselves. We create and leave a wake behind. Everyone was disappointed. However, she understood that was the consequence to her actions and my decision. There are always consequences.

Leading sacrificially means being mindful of giving false warnings, neglecting boundaries, and the awareness of consequences. *Setting standards and holding true to them foster learning, awareness, and growth.* Development is often accompanied by discomfort. Leaders should aspire to the moment where sacrifice is the difficult road before them; it's in that moment that they have the opportunity to inspire people to grow. Be the enforcer of integrity.

Sacrificial Intention

Our culture says, "Do what's best for you. Do what makes you *feel* good. Follow your heart. Self-promote." *Your* this, *your* that, *your* truth, *I, me, my* ... To those for whom that rings true, what an incredible, lonely divide that creates. Leading with emotion is not the same as leading with passion, nor does it accomplish the same results. We're all on this earth together, living our lives, but what if we flipped the current narrative and decided to *serve others*? What if we put ourselves in check and decided to intentionally know another's story first rather than put ourselves in the forefront of every circumstance? What if we assumed good intentions rather than drawing a short line to hate? If we focused on sacrificial leadership, this whole world would look different. Taking the *you* out of any situation yields so many benefits!

Being sacrificial is the right thing to do—the fruitful thing to do—but it requires understanding, intention, and practice. When something is not easy, our culture right now quickly affirms, even encourages us, to not take that route, regardless of whether it's the best path. It's because the word itself is intimidating. But lost words like *sacrifice, accountability, responsibility, ownership*, and just plain *wrong* build character in us all. They build perseverance. They foster growth. They also enable respect to coexist with *disagreement* (an important component). These words distinguish leaders and build a stronger community, both in business and in our personal lives and neighborhoods.

It's OK to disagree. It's common, necessary, and even *innovative* to disagree. It might surprise you, but entering into a disagreement is also sacrificial. You could turn away, but if we agreed on everything, life would be less meaningful. The hard way is sometimes the best way. Leading sacrificially opens the door to the greatest growth of all.

Effort is sacrificial. Taking the time to understand others is sacrificial. Taking the time to grow as a person is, as well.

As with anything in difficult or growth-oriented leadership, intentional effort and actions are required. Sacrifice is often not the easy road, but it's the path that takes us where we need to go. My daughter still remembers that summer afternoon. We were both upset, but I have seen people in parenting and leadership roles who shy away from this kind of sacrifice. They won't deal with conflict or challenges. They'll either issue idle threats, which don't give them much credibility, or they won't do anything at all. I could have let it slide to get to that party, but that wasn't in the best interest of my daughter. It took willingness on my part to sacrifice what *I* wanted. Today, witnessing the marvelous young woman she has become, I'm glad I made that decision and countless others.

When we hold others accountable, we teach them to see outside themselves and learn from their mistakes. This even means intentionally acting with restraint—stepping away and watching someone learn the hard lessons without your provision of a soft landing. Leading sacrificially takes focus, strength, and a key discernment of how *others* will benefit. I see this sacrificial piece as something many leaders, and people in general, aren't willing to lean into. There is a hesitancy to give up their ability to step out of conflict. Either people are unwilling to *give* or it's *too hard*. They also covet being popular or being perceived as kind. Yet, kindness isn't telling people what they want to hear or leaving them where they are just because it makes *you* feel good. Kindness is generous and considerate; it actually is being generous of yourself and considerate toward their development and awareness. Their focus is on the wrong person. It's on themselves and not others. Leadership shines brightest in the face of opposition, not in the ease of popular opinion.

The sacrificial lens means giving up something of worth to you for the sake of advancing others. Perhaps it seems daunting, but it's also very simple, and simple doesn't necessarily equate to easy. Simple just makes the answer or the end goal clear.

Sacrificial Teaching

Teaching can be sacrificial when done the right way. If you're a seasoned teacher, whether at a school, in ministry, or in a corporate setting, then the efficiency is often already there—curriculum, schedule, tests, etc. You may not want to give up this efficiency because it's quick and easy. The problem is that there's a simplistic *framework* embedded in teaching. Almost like it's a task. Changing modes and digging deeper into those coaching, mentoring, and teaching moments, you finally see that the act of teaching is more important than the task itself. To embrace this shift, you need to reshape your mind.

Truly investing in those you teach, knowing how much value *slowing down* brings to their lives, means sacrificing other things you need to get done, plain and simple. Sacrificing current priorities for a new priority—the individual you're investing in for the sake of their future—this is leading for impact. Sacrificing efficiency now (the "I can do it faster myself" attitude), for someone else's efficiency later, carries mutual benefits. This effort, this mind shift, is also an investment in *your values*. The outward lens shows you that what you put into others has a direct benefit for you, too. Think about a new employee who wasn't given enough instruction or, worse yet, sits around idle. It's hard to motivate them on a new learning path if they don't feel that connection and support. They're probably thinking, "I don't know what I'm doing and no one's helping me. Am I worth being here? Is my position important?" They *are* important. Sacrifice until you no longer see it as a sacrifice.

You know the phenomenon: there are leaders who know things that they don't want to share. They fear that they're sacrificing time and knowledge, or they fear competition. This is a fallacy. You never sacrifice knowledge—you're always sharing it. And perhaps you have a hundred other things you need to do (tasks that would better serve *you*), but *sacrificial teaching and mentorship require taking the time to give that person what they need, giving them the tools for success and growth.* Sometimes people don't want these tools, and that's OK. I think of this from a faith perspective. If God did everything for me that I *wanted*, I wouldn't be in a very good place. But I'm given what I *need*—what is necessary—and oftentimes what I receive is contrary to what I want. A *need* propels me forward, over a *want* that merely brings momentary gratification.

My leadership position in ministry was a sacrifice initially. I wouldn't go out on Friday nights because I had early morning ministry on Saturdays. I gave up coed flag football and Monday night football games to attend Bible study. In return, my life was enriched tenfold, and those "sacrifices" were replaced with real-life blessings in abundance. You recall my story with the youth. Thirteen or so years later, I was privileged to serve in a substitute teaching leadership position where I was called upon and equipped to welcome new members, lead groups, teach seminars, train leaders, and give out lectures.

Approaching that role, I thought, "Not a chance in this world. You've got the wrong Jennifer again." That's not how a calling works. It is a privilege and an awesome, humble revelation that you were appointed to something meaningful. I was chosen; in spite of who I am, in spite of what I cannot do on my own, and in spite of *me*, I was chosen. You set yourself aside and faithfully walk in readiness and trust. You don't get to pick and choose what you want, but you can be sacrificial with what you receive because you know that it's for your good and for a greater purpose—one beyond yourself. I was called upon to grow as a leader. In terms of ministry, I needed to consistently make sacrifices several times a week to show my devotion, learn about people, and fully grasp compassion, which was part of my equipping and a great challenge to set myself, my opinion, and my desires aside.

It's not the road I would have chosen. When I looked at it from the outside world, all I would have seen was giving up what I enjoyed. Now I see very clearly that it was exactly what I needed to replace my momentary, fleeting pleasures with lasting joy, discipline, and rich devotion. Returning to parenting, you look at a child and know what they need. Yeah, sometimes they don't want to eat. They don't want fruits and vegetables, but they'll accept a cookie. It's the same in your leadership role. There will be things you would rather do in the face of things that aren't your favorite. Still, we have to get the difficult things done. If you've been called upon to be a leader, you've also been called upon to be a teacher, coach, mentor, and steward over others, influencing them toward the "need" over the "want."

Being a faithful steward over others is sacrificial. It goes past the time and devotion you put in to expand their skills and knowledge. It's about what is truly best for them in business and beyond. In a market where the right talent is difficult to find and retain (which actually can be the case in many different markets for different reasons), businesses and leaders arguably have a sacrificial outlook in that they would retain "good people/workers" at all costs and do whatever it takes. The problem in this scenario is that a good concept is being applied in the wrong way.

Yes, people are our most valuable asset, but the *keep at all costs* concept assumes your business is the right place for them, which just may not be the case. I believe that when someone is ready to leave, and it's right for them, then it inherently is the best decision for the company as well. There have been a few occasions when someone I respected and appreciated came to me to have the "other opportunity" discussion. In those moments, the sacrificial action for me was to let them go and facilitate a celebratory and gracious exit, not to do whatever it takes to keep them to myself, though I may want to.

In those times, the need to set yourself aside for the benefit of seeing their path clearly is very important. To coach them through the tough decision by championing their path, and coming alongside them with the purest motivation, is fulfilling. If the next step in their career is elsewhere, I will not be one to hold them back. I will be the first to encourage them and celebrate their steps. In a company about people, it truly is less about "me" and more about "you."

Sacrificial Effort

Effort is sacrificial. It shouldn't be! We all should want to make an effort to help each other. Effort should be a *requirement*, similar to being taught to do the right thing. In our times, culturally, it's become sacrificial because we have to step away from being consumed by our own lives.

I have participated in programs where high-level experts gave their time and talent to teach and educate—providing an opportunity for business leaders to get ahead of the game, see what's coming, and do something for the good of their companies. Many leaders in this program were CEOs from across the nation. There were leaders whose predominant outlook was "Well, what is this going to do for me?

What will it give me? How do I benefit?" I knew immediately that these colleagues were missing the point.

These leading experts in their skilled arenas were sacrificing their time, talent, and expertise to educate, and the information they provided was brilliant. They were sacrificially positioning companies to gain a competitive advantage and protect themselves. There were leaders who couldn't see the incredible opportunity that was laid before them. They were waiting for everything to fall into their laps. Yes, it would take effort to implement what we were taught, but a proper perspective would view that effort as an opportunity. There are many businesses that haven't yet had a chance to participate in the readiness program that we engaged in. I viewed it as being given a gift, while others were saying, "That's too much work," or "I don't think I need that." The phenomenon was baffling but far too common today.

Countless times, I've been in meetings where other business owners and leaders expect that they deserve to be freely given something. What happened to merit? They fail to recognize or have gratitude for opportunities, and instead they want something tangible like a contract or a reward. With any opportunity in life, what you make of it is up to you. *The opposite of effort is entitlement and expectation.* Please understand that in any opportunity, there are other people *wanting* for that same moment. *Effort is sacrificial, and so is gratitude.*

I also had the privilege to meet with representatives from different corporate partners in an open forum. During the conversation, I asked what their expectations were for engaging new business partnerships, essentially what was important and valuable to *them.* This approach would enable me to then assess and advocate well for a mutually beneficial relationship. After asking these questions, a gentleman at the table responded, "I'm so glad you said that. Do you know how many times people demand, 'Well, what contract will you give me? Where will this get me?'" I couldn't agree with him more.

Our society suffers from an entitled mentality. There are those who are unwilling to put in the effort—the sacrifice—and are unable to appreciate the opportunities before them. *Effort, sacrifice, ambition, and a solid business are the prerequisites to engage in any opportunity.* Don't be so consumed by your real or perceived barriers that you can't recognize the lever in front of you waiting for you to pull it. Seize every opportunity, fail forward, and pull that lever again until you succeed.

Let's return to the missing piece: relational relevance. Relationship building. Owners and managers want instant gratification in their businesses while neglecting to invest in relationships. It's remarkable to see this in business-to-business interactions. No matter your position, no one should expect to be handed something without intending to establish a relationship. Building relationships takes time and intentional effort, especially in big companies. People often dismiss the fact that relationships are the glue that holds everything together and fosters growth. It takes great sacrifice.

At Summit Group, I'm not willing to engage in unethical business practices or actions that have the potential for detrimental impacts to individuals. That means we'll miss out on some business opportunities, but this is the *sacrifice* that we make to stay true to our values and reputation. Leading for impact focuses on values, integrity, and doing the right thing, even if you "lose" in the eyes of culture. The secret is that you'll never lose. You're guided by your North Star—truth.

Your moral center is always a strong guide, and it requires an open-handed embrace. Leading sacrificially takes hold of every opportunity with effort and appreciation. Managing and leading sacrificially leaves your own fears and discomforts at the door and enables you to enter into a supportive and strengthening role for the benefit of another rather than your own. Sacrifice in leadership should be something you strive for, something you teach by example, and something you just do.

Leading Sacrificially

Sacrificial leading means giving up something of worth to you for the sake of advancing others.

SPARKS OF TRUTH

- Sacrificial leadership sets self aside and upholds others.

- Sacrificial leading requires strong intention and discipline—in thought, attitude, and action.

- Sacrificial leading requires integrity: doing what is right, even in the face of opposition.

- Sacrifice until you no longer view it as a sacrifice.

PROMPTS FOR IMPACT

- Share a story of how you benefited from someone else's sacrificial leadership.

- How are you prompted to be more sacrificial in your leadership?

NOTES

....

....

....

....

....

....

....

....

....

....

....

....

....

....

Letting go means to come to the realization that some people are a part of your history, but not a part of your destiny.

—STEVE MARABOLI

CHAPTER SIX

Open-Handed Embrace

open-handed: giving freely; generous.

embrace: accept or support willingly and enthusiastically.

Visualize a fist versus an open palm. A fist closes tightly, maybe to hide something or keep something from someone else. It's associated with the use of force. If you imagine a leader ruling with a fist, you might expect directives over collaboration, even harshness or being unwelcoming. An open hand, however, is nonthreatening, often offered as a handshake, introduction, or a "good to see you." Offering a palm up suggests a willingness to assist or help—"take my hand" or "let me support you." An open hand dovetails well with an embrace because it reinforces willing support, even acceptance, which is important to much of the workforce today.

An open-handed embrace approach as a leader means that you give of yourself generously to support your staff enthusiastically and genuinely. You are eager to do what is necessary to help them soar, even if that means them soaring away from you to thrive somewhere new.

In any leadership role, it's incredibly gratifying to watch people grow and thrive. Ultimately, there are times when that means spreading their wings and leaving their positions under your leading yet with your encouragement and allowance. There are also others who you pour into, but they go their own way and you know it's best to support a separation and exit. An open-handed embrace means relying on your values to discern the right thing to do—to reward when there is a chance to reward and to send off well when the time presents itself.

As a leader, if you honor others and uphold your values, letting go is not complicated. It doesn't matter if they appreciate you, nor does it matter if, in their ignorance or lack of experience, they speak poorly of you or fail to appreciate what you've done. It only matters that you've led them well.

You'll recall from Leading Sacrificially that the decisions you make are about others and not yourself. It starts with the employee—who they are, where they are, and then where you want to take them (if they are willing to go). It requires meeting them at the exact place they stand, at any given moment in time, and then being intentional about how you want them to prosper. Embrace them, and then create a plan that you both can follow through on. These are all steps that a lot of managers don't do or don't do well. They're not interested or invested enough in their people. Some leaders consider this kind of work outside the scope of their role. The truth is that pouring into others without knowing the outcome is leading for impact—doing the right thing, whatever the cost and regardless of the benefit to you.

A leader in their fullness is a mentor and a coach. We have a high calling and privilege to do both. We coach to help a person reach their full potential and succeed in their role. We mentor to prioritize the person's advancement and career development. The latter goes beyond performance and enhances the realm of relationship. We engage with the employee's career through sharing our knowledge, skills, and experience to participate in their growth and long-term success.

A guidepost I share with my management team through our values is to be rooted in truth and the desire to cause each person to flourish and lack nothing—refine through vulnerability with the goal of upholding who the person is and their potential in their current role and beyond. Letting someone fail is neither honoring nor kind. Respect is admiring them for who they are and having confidence in their ability to excel through every obstacle. The action of mentoring invests in and embraces those that you lead. Once you commit to investing in another and initiate action, it becomes their responsibility to receive and execute. Not everyone will. Not everyone is ready. Not everyone was meant to respond. Do what you intend and what you can, and then let go.

Sometimes I think that is part of what is humbling. We are the leaders but not of another's life. Only *they* are in charge of that. However, we can *influence* them in a manner that empowers and refines them. There are no guarantees with people, but the very act of welcoming someone and walking beside them could be their key to continued success. Within this act of service, you can't always hold on, but it's not your choice to make. Give without expectation. Always be prepared to celebrate or to walk away and wish them well.

Lifting Others

When you lead for impact, it is simple to influence with integrity—wanting the best for someone else, while also setting yourself aside. An open-handed embrace brings to mind two employees, both of whom were vital colleagues and team members at our company. One was in operations, and the other was on the general and administrative (G&A) side of the business. They were both strong assets to our team, well liked and incredibly loyal!

The operations person was with us for over six years. We were her first stop in the professional realm right out of college, and she strongly embodied our values from the start. She loved to coach, teach, and train. Yet, I could see the burden she carried, and we had serious conversations about what her career looked like—what was the next phase for her. Eventually, she decided it was time to experience and engage in a career/life outside of our team. She needed to let go of the burden and see the opportunities awaiting her because of her talent and incredible character. The realization was hard for both of us.

We chose to invest in her future instead of dangling temporary carrots that may work for a time of distraction but never address the core of her important journey. Letting go is bittersweet, but just as a parent watches their own leave the security of home and forge their own paths, this is the same. It was clear that the time was right to move on. She proceeded to a large enterprise and thrived. Today, she's in another great role with a fantastic company. Her life is blessed, her success continues to build, and she is still an important part of our lives and our company's history. *Joy is greater when you invest in people; celebrating them is always the reward.* She had become part of the family inside and outside of work, but deep down, I needed to encourage her to grow, and to *go*, with an open-handed embrace.

The second example of an open-handed embrace involved our G&A wizard. She had been with us for over four years—intelligent, talented, hilarious, and committed to our team and our values. She was someone whom I trusted and sought out for the position. Multiple times she generously stated that I was her mentor, and I promised her that because of that, I would always be here, as a sounding board, an encourager, and a truth-teller.

When we discussed the opportunity to move on and step into an industry she was passionate about, I asked her what she loved the most here, and her response made my heart sing: *It was the people. Our team!* I challenged her to be the light in a new environment and create her own value-driven team bond. As she talked around what she did and did not know about this new role, I very calmly settled into the discernment that this was her next step—with challenges and rewards, and hopefully, with growth. Don't get me wrong, I wasn't thrilled. I was deeply saddened, but it wasn't about me. There were a dozen reasons I could throw at her to stay, but instead, I gave her this: "If you tell me that the money is important, then I'll counter and beat them. I'll bend over backward. But I don't know that that's the right thing for you. We can't offer you the same growth in that field of interest."

If you look for reasons to stay or delay, they are easy to find. What we walked through was setting Summit Group and timing aside (there's never a "good" time to leave in accounting/finance) and, instead, focused solely on what was attractive about her new offer and how that would impact her career. It was a good move. I had the chance to visit her when I was in town, and she dropped by the office to see everyone. Hugs, tears, and celebration were affirmations that we did something selfless and bold together.

Ultimately, an open-handed embrace is most challenging when letting go of the good ones—the hardworking, values-driven employees who feel like family. Don't cling to them though. Sacrificially let go. I know it's hard, but I know also when it's right. *Embrace with open hands, teach and mentor with clarity and conviction, and then release with an open heart.* An open-handed embrace is selfless. There will always be different opportunities for people. Make sure that if they stay, it's for the right reasons and contributes to both the person's career and the health of your company.

Letting go is easier said than done. You can pour yourself into people completely, coach them, and do everything you can, but they may still need or want to go elsewhere. As the saying goes, "If you love them, let them go." And sometimes they do come back! We've had the blessing of team members return to us. It brings an abundance of joy to receive them again and continue to watch them thrive in new and bigger ways.

If you're currently walking through a new opportunity with an important team member, commit to an open discussion together. As a leader, be generous in your approach:

1. Set the tone. Listen well with an open heart and mind.

2. Be a selfless advocate. What's best for the employee, ultimately, is what's best for the company too.

3. Be interested. Consider the following questions to spark your conversation:

    ‣ What do you value here that you would miss?

    ‣ What are you looking forward to in the new role?

    ‣ Would fixing something here create the same opportunity?

▸ How would you like me to support you in this decision?

Letting Go

Letting go of people is part of business. Especially in this new workforce, there are fewer legacy employees. Some are sent off to prosper; others must be sent on by *necessity*. I'll preface this by saying: We don't fully know what other factors are at play in our employees' lives—only what they are willing to share. We see a glimpse of a life lived before us; sometimes there may be unshared struggles or unspoken forces of influence we don't know or see. What I do know is that the more people are lacking in their own role, the worse they become in every other area, and their focus begins to creep into spheres they know little of in an effort to distract and deflect from the accountability of their own performance. It rots a person's character.

Lacking in responsibility only gets uglier as the situation muddies itself—performance, relationships, attitudes, and the like decline and have a heavy impact on culture. This is why one of the first things I like to do is encourage people to be vulnerable so that we don't make assumptions or decisions in a vacuum. However, some are unwilling and unable to get there. Regardless of the level of sharing, there is a new level of teaching needed regarding personal responsibility versus employer responsibility. In the age of start-ups, tech companies, and employee care, this has been mistranslated and misunderstood by many.

I try to catch things early and work with people, creating a transformative plan to execute together. Ultimately, the most effective communication is in-person so that intention is clear, points are covered respectfully, and there is an opportunity to dialogue through it together. I firmly believe that no one should be surprised when they're terminated. In our company, the walk to the door is thoughtful and drenched with recovery opportunities because I've communicated with them and have followed through with a plan to make it right. If the next stage is termination, I try to get them there before the bitterness and resentment permeate through the team. Sometimes you just can't avoid where they are at emotionally or what their personal lives bleed into their professional selves. Let them go.

In recent years, we brought someone on who displayed great communication, contagious positivity, and maturity throughout the interview process. We extended multiple accommodations including remote work, flexible hours, and extensive time off. In the end, we *struggled* with this relationship. It became evident that their knowledge, performance, and, most important, their lack of integrity and commitment to *our* values hung by a thread. Interestingly enough, being positive was the pride of life for this person, but every action and inaction told a different story.

After their departure, I reached out to take the person to lunch to discuss comments made at exit that were never communicated prior, and actually had little validity, but were due more to a lack of business understanding. I was willing to meet them in whatever space of discontent there was and walk them to a place of growth and even enjoy a nice lunch. I never received a response. Not a professional decline or acknowledgment, nothing. I've been around enough to know when someone just wants to complain versus reconcile, but it's my job to offer an opportunity to find resolution. I did what I needed to do to walk away with a clear conscience and present an opportunity to reconcile. It matters not whether the other person engages. That is always the hope but sometimes not the reality. This is an employee who didn't have the bandwidth to do the job, wasn't honoring the values, and sadly, couldn't own their own lack of performance.

A common response by poor performers is that they project themselves into arenas they know little about and find things to complain about—it's deflection. From my experienced point of view, they don't realize how much their lack of maturity in professionalism and experiences shines through in those moments, and some don't particularly even care. What they also don't realize, at least at the time, is that those things follow them. The tools and support were there, but the timing perhaps wasn't right. You see the potential they have, but they're nowhere near reaching it, or they're sliding backward because of their own choices and lack of perspective. The alignment is not right.

An open-handed embrace allows us to let go of someone who doesn't want to grow. It releases judgment because at the end of the day, regardless of their performance, we are not a good fit for them. It is, however, a lesson in time, meaningful to both parties. I have gratitude for those times, and I can find things about the person that are positive, that are endearing, and that I respect. Problematic employees often present a clear pattern in their behavior. They find faults outside of themselves instead of choosing to grow within.

These employees require an open-handed embrace because you have to let go. The residual sting must be minimized. Part with them before they become toxic to the culture. Above all, the *culture* is what I'm here to protect. The bad situations hurt me much more because of the fundamental importance of values as our bedrock. When you see someone not adhere to these values—even though we go to great lengths to discuss them—it's a huge blow. But on the values front, I know we are on solid ground. My hope for each of the difficult experiences is that humility replaces pride and mentorship replaces self-blinded actions.

As a leader, in times of disappointment, I remind myself that it's not my life and not my place to scrutinize *their* life and journey—where they are, where they're going, where they need protection, and where they're hurting. If they let me in, it's far easier to stand beside them and navigate forward together, but again, it is not a right of mine to exercise; it's a privilege they allow or disallow. An open-handed embrace reminds me that my job is to give freely and let them receive everything, receive a little bit, or throw it all away. This process of letting go is healthy; it makes room for someone else who's ready to come in and give their all.

Surviving Change

Leaders and managers can agree on the rising tide of the self-focused worker—one who assumes their value for the company exists in spades and it is the company alone that owes them something—something beyond the contractual obligation. The rise of big tech and start-up-funded playgrounds at work helped to create an imbalance and misunderstanding of professional worth and work ethic. The voice of a few large enterprises has created a perception of normalcy that is not shared by all.

From the media standpoint, one would assume there were a solid few that dominate the world, when, in fact, there are significantly more small and midsize companies that contribute to employment and job growth and influence productive members of society. They may not provide meals and snacks, unlimited time off, or salaries far above industry and skill standard, but they have a very real impact reach. These small and midsize companies embrace the fabric of our communities, and many of these businesses have been, and remain, devoted to the people beyond the dollar.

In the recent workforce, I have been amazed at the number of professionals who lack mentors. Instead, they thrive on "groupthink" and seek out a like-minded community lacking experience but are experts at making one another feel good in the moment. Groupthink diminishes the effectiveness of truly collaborative environments. It works to discourage individual creativity, responsibility, and development. We all love our champions and affirmations, but the courageous pursuit of professional growth distinguishes future leaders and current leadership. It's not the job-hopping itself that is an issue; it's the underlying reasons for why they leave—there isn't staying power because skills and growth are lacking. Among the field of recruiters, I see a large gap in skill and experience that is poorly reflected in compensation. Ability is being outshined by uncorroborated pay scales, fancy titles, and so on. Leaders need to commit to their own continued education and pour into their work teams.

We are coming out of a time where many were privileged to work from home, while too many weren't afforded the same opportunities. Livelihoods were uprooted, and there was, and remains, tremendous loss, but some people were afforded the pendulum ride of the times. As business profits sink and markets shift, the layoffs from the giants began to travel through the professional realm. Social and professional networks became a place of venting and opinion-bearing for many. Only, it was often layered in blame and entitlement rather than gratitude and growth.

Gone are the days of mutual contract. Employees want more and *seemingly* give less—this is a broad-brush stroke but suffice it to note that if in fact they do give less, it's for the lack of leadership and accountability. We get what we allow and create, in the manner in which we lead. Companies must shift focus to educate more on liabilities, values, and people-centric investments to preserve a mutually beneficial engagement. We need to fix the imbalance together, which means being realistic about where you are, what you want, and what you are worth (skills, not dignity). For companies, the same—what you are looking for, what you expect, and what you can provide.

A good place to start is with the person's professional makeup. What experience and skills do they bring with them, and are these pertinent to the role? Expecting a company pay based on desired lifestyle or on a noncomparable situation is unrealistic. One candidate was interested in a role that he certainly could do, but he wanted to be compensated for all his other skills and experiences that were not relevant to or part of the role. If I applied for an accounting role, I could make a case that I was qualified, but if I layered in that I expected compensation for also being a CEO, I would be laughed out of the building. Any skills outside of those necessary for the role are irrelevant.

There was another recent candidate who set a salary expectation that wasn't reflective of the market or their skills in relation to the role. The process stalled when the individual wanted a salary based on the affluent area where they *desired* to find an apartment or purchase a home—essentially, the candidate wanted us to pay a premium to enable a savvier lifestyle, regardless of the market value of their skill set in the given area. In the end, the candidate wanted what they wanted, and we parted ways. There is a sense of worth that is great from a confidence perspective but is terribly unrealistic and out of balance, in fact detrimental, now and in the long run.

Entitlement is a breeding ground for destructive strongholds. It's important to understand that markets shift. We've had a long run of candidate-driven demands, but now the scale is rebalancing itself.

Leaders should be in tune to market changes to help educate and navigate through candidate and employee demands, interests, and rewards that make them feel valued. Hold on to what works but not so tightly that when there is a shift, big or small, it pulls you into an uncompetitive space. Be open-handed so that you see the shifts from different perspectives and are able to decide for yourself where you want to stand and how you will help others navigate through it as well.

There's *entitlement* in our culture today. It frustrates me to no end when modern workers don't look at things from an employer's standpoint in their given field and also when companies become irate and refuse to hear what is most important to the individual job seekers. *It's not your job to meet the potential employee's wish list at every level, especially the personal preferences outside of relevant needs. It is, however, a leader's responsibility to narrow the divide by engaging in compromise and education and to communicate professionally what you are able and willing to provide.*

A note to employees: If you have a tax issue, seek advice from certified tax professionals. If it's a salary divide, use reliable salary sources that are verified by HR professionals rather than just an online site where anyone can boast about what they are supposedly being paid. Gather all the information important to you, and look at compensation as a whole (salary, benefits, etc.). Approach the situation with information so that you don't make demands that may prove unreasonable.

Employers, don't dismiss what's important to the individual. To both, reputation follows you *everywhere*. Be respectful and kind, even if it means the chairs at the table are on absolute opposing ends. You each have an easy solution. Find a different table! Smile warmly, have gratitude for the experience, and part ways before the ugly has time to surface. In time, you may be proven both right and wrong.

Grace to Self

Self-reflection, affirming your values, and doing your best are all components of having an open-handed embrace for yourself, too. Recognize when you're at different points of divide with people. Affirm to yourself that as long as your conscience is clear, you've done what you could do, *needed* to do, and you have to let it go. You can't torture yourself about what may or may not happen. You can only do what is in your realm of control. To keep yourself accountable, ask yourself these questions:

- Did I uphold my commitment to our values?

- Did I honor the other person and their potential?

- Did I listen and properly discern what action was needed to benefit them?

- Did I act with integrity in doing what I communicated I would?

- Did I hold them accountable to the pursuit of professional development?

You can't give everything, but you can give generously. You must not expect that the other person will necessarily *receive* everything or even give in return. I tell my accounting team, "We're *looking for excellence, not perfection. Because we'll always fall short of perfection in every aspect of our lives—whatever we do—but we can still work with excellence.*" If you can tell yourself, "I operated with excellence in this space," then you've done well enough in that moment.

An open-handed embrace with yourself couldn't be possible if not through a values-driven lens. If you're doing what needs to be done to say that you did it right, *within yourself,* then that is a good place to stand among opposition. As leaders, we offer a lot to others, constantly giving out and being taken from, but there's not the same level of reciprocation or pouring into *you*. It's not anyone else's job to give as much as you do. That is why taking care of yourself is so important. Indeed, it can be lonely at the top, so part of your accountability is to surround yourself with a strong CEO group, a board, advisors, and mentors of your own—lead by example. You are responsible for *you*. The better you are, the more you can give.

What you learned in Leading Sacrificially was the ideal—the path that some of the greatest leaders of all time have followed. The open-handed embrace brings us down to earth. The reality is that even the most sacrificial leader will have difficult decisions and tough losses. As you know, it's a dance—a balance—and embracing others while keeping the door open is important for people to naturally flow in and out and to *re*balance.

I had an auntie in Hawai'i who used to say, "The bad days make the good days seem even better." I never forgot her words. If everything in life were so grand all the time, life would lose its luster, and we wouldn't appreciate the challenges and the downtimes. We would most certainly lack perspective. We must embrace the *practical*.

These challenging experiences are beneficial and refining, preparing us to appreciate those bright moments even more. Lead sacrificially, and also recognize that we're all human and encounter each other at different points in life. Give everyone, including yourself, an open-handed embrace.

Open-Handed Embrace

An open-handed embrace approach means giving generously to afford another's growth and success, even if it means letting go.

SPARKS OF TRUTH

- An open-handed embrace is selfless.

- There are no guarantees with people; walk beside them anyway.

- Part with problematic employees before they become toxic to your culture.

- A leader to follow commits to their own development to effectively pour into others.

- You are responsible for *you.* Let others bear responsibility for themselves.

PROMPTS FOR IMPACT

- Share a time when someone was part of your journey but not your destiny.

- Identify a professional situation that is good, bad, or even ugly right now. How will you commit to walk through it with an open-handed embrace?

NOTES

....

....

....

....

....

....

....

....

....

....

....

....

....

....

....

The ultimate measure
of a man is not
where he stands in
moments of comfort
and convenience but
where he stands at
times of challenge
and controversy.

—DR. MARTIN LUTHER KING

CHAPTER SEVEN

Discerning Disruption

discerning: seeing and understanding clearly and intelligently.

disruption: disturbance or problems that interrupt an event, activity, or process.

Discernment, as the aforementioned definition suggests, is a form of knowing. It's that ability to soundly judge, to *see, sense, and feel* things without someone necessarily speaking about the issue specifically. It's the ability to assess through *awareness, observation, or connection.*

Disruption is any kind of change, which is often necessary. There's a negative connotation to the word *disruption*, but it's important to remember that the only constant is change. Things are changing all the time, but when the changes are bigger, people tend to notice them more, and their responses can fall anywhere along a spectrum of reactions. Many of us go to a natural stress response, while others seem unfazed, even unimpacted. A leader's impact is significant in times of uncertainty and disruption, and it is the leader's discernment and action that influence whether it's navigated well.

Disruption tends to naturally stir up some level of concern. Our *culture* makes the idea of change big and dramatic. Consider reality television shows where daily life is magnified and its purpose to stir up situations that involve conflict, high emotion, or divisive interests. People seem drawn to disruption, sometimes in a good way—unifying, supporting, resolving together—other times bringing judgment, divisiveness, and chaos.

Hurricanes and other natural disasters illustrate the progression of the human response. They draw people together in preparation and readiness, stirring up collective fear in anticipation, chaos in experience, devastation in damage and loss, and then they bring us back to community healing in the wake. Life is going to serve change, and sometimes that disruption is not going to be welcomed, so be the leader to follow and show your teams how to lean into those circumstances rather than work to try to escape them—perseverance builds character. Discernment, applied wisely, fosters preparation, perseverance, and prosperity.

In historical accounts of discerning disruption, I look at the life of the apostle Paul (formerly, Saul). Here is an educated man who led the intense persecution and destruction of the early church, dragging men and women off to prison. Yet, on the road to Damascus, his life would forever be transformed. He became one of the most influential leaders of his time, and beyond, bringing the gospel to the Gentile world. Even so, Paul, in his letter to Timothy, declares himself the worst of sinners (1 Timothy 1:15). His transformed life was not lived in comfort or worldly pleasures. Rather, it was marked by extraordinary suffering—imprisoned, flogged, exposed to death repeatedly, received "forty lashes," beaten with rods, stoned, shipwrecked, constantly on the move, in danger, sleep deprived, hungry and thirsty, cold and naked ... (2 Corinthians 11:16–33)—more than most of us could "boast" at our worst.

During this persecution, Paul executed his greatest purpose with love and conviction. In spite of strong opposition, never did he use flattery—he did not seek the praise of men. Paul worked day and night in order not to be a burden to anyone. Instead, he encouraged, strengthened, and served others, considering them with precious joy as he persevered in the purpose entrusted to him. His discernment regarding the struggles of those he sought to serve and the circumstances that would befall him was executed upon with great wisdom and discipline yet with gratitude and humility. Paul is a leader for impact while discerning disruption. He served in fullest capacity to transform the lives of others.

In our present day, we deal with a magnitude of change that is happening simultaneously in our collective lives—across the nation and the world. Every generation experiences a different set of disruptions. Ours has certainly been filled with those of our own making. As I reflect on major events in my post-collegiate years, the economic gut punches stand out: the dot-com boom in early 2000s, the housing crisis in 2008, COVID-19 responses in 2020, and the predictions of the current recessionary pressure as well as the predictions of the coming depression in the 2030s. It's hard not to notice the indicators ripe for downturn in our current market: overvaluations, lavish spending/living above your means, active venture capital investments, media involvement, lack of individual discovery and discernment, uncertainty, and unrest.

As I see it, our current state promptly and actively is issuing its warnings; it's just a matter of time before a new reality comes to fruition. Broadening our scope away from just the economic indicators, we have accelerating factors in our midst: technological innovation and generative artificial intelligence (AI), rapid new wealth upended by homelessness and poverty, political unrest, and so forth. We most certainly have a monster on our hands. Rapid change is happening all around us, with only signs of continued acceleration. This can easily distort our ability to discern—to reflect upon these changes, prepare appropriately, and come to them from an intelligent and values-based perspective. The impact is far-reaching; it's a time of rapid, brilliant advancement with global impact, and it must be met with leaders who can discern disruption, lean in, and navigate through it.

In the face of rapid change, there's one thing that we can control: how we lead (preparation and response). Having the ability to discern when disruption is rearing its head and then moving toward action—especially, getting in front of it—is an active response toward resolution. Successfully discerning disruption relies upon the principles of Leading for Impact—acknowledging how something intersects with your values, growth, and prosperity, personally and professionally.

If we start with our values, anytime something bumps against them, we hold on to our core and let go of (or dislodge) what's threatening our foundation. There will be continual disruption in business and in life, and leaders are called to be vigilant, alert, and responsive. We protect our bedrock first and foremost by using discernment to act in the best interests of our people and our companies.

Commitment

We're all living this life together, and not once has life given me an indication that this is going to be a smooth ride, but in every circumstance lies a chance to lead, grow, and succeed. This is where being principled is important. As a leader, your firm foundation is a beacon, and others on shifting sand, in time, will wither away. Like Paul, humility and perseverance are essential as well as the mindset and continual action to serve others. Leaders suffer well when they uphold their commitment to those they serve and endure without bitterness the burden of their own circumstances. When your team sees you encounter and thrive through hardship, their confidence in you grows. As a leader, you need to establish your sounding board and solid ground. You need to be an example of how to walk through whatever life throws your way and come out strong on the other side.

Authentic commitment to your people and values means that you always know what to do. In times of uncertainty and disruption, people are naturally very good at creating our *own* chaos magnifiers that stray from progress and resolution. It's not that we'll do it perfectly every time, but the commitment to others and alignment to our values are what drive us home. The only constant is change, and within that change, we are the calm within the storm, the steady ground, and the safe place to rest. Remain vigilant during any time of adjustment—whether perceived as good or bad—and follow this golden rule: communicate, communicate, communicate!

Communication

Relational beings need to communicate. In celebration or in crisis, communication bonds us together. Whether a disruption is good or bad, small or large, a leader's manner and level of communication is a key indicator of adaption and recovery, of synergy and effectiveness. There is not a single person I know who does not understand the importance of communication, yet it is an area that often becomes a stumbling block, especially in crisis. During times of uncertainty, the response and action of a discerning leader is the stepping stone for others to navigate well through it. Here are key communication pillars to remember:

1. *Communicate Urgently:* Get in front of the event or issue, or someone else will. Control the chaos, or the chaos will magnify the disruption. Urgency lets people know you value them and won't leave them behind. It doesn't have to be long or informative initially, but you should include the following:

   ▸ State what's happening and its known impact.

   ▸ Share your plan of action to manage your response and its impact.

   ▸ Let them know what you need—for example, "Right now it's critical to direct my time and attention to response planning."

   ▸ Give them assurance that you will keep them informed.

   ▸ Let them know when you will update them next.

   ▸ Thank them for partnering with you, and let them know you are committed to doing what is right and best for them and the company.

2. *Communicate with a Unified Voice:* Don't go this alone. Loop in your management team quickly. Make sure everyone is comfortable and equipped to articulate the same message. This unity will build confidence and trust among your team. Let them hear directly from you, the CEO, or leader of your team or organization, as often as possible.

3. *Communicate Clearly:* Be concise and clear in every message you deliver. Stay focused on what is happening

and what needs to get done. Restate your commitment, and share the resources you have supporting you. Acknowledge areas that are unknown, and let them know that when you have more information, you will readily share that with them.

4. *Communicate Often:* Overcommunication is far better than undercommunicating, especially in a crisis. Do not leave people to their imaginations—this is not the space and time for an innovative mindset. If possible, set an expectation for the frequency of updates you are able to give, being upfront that as things evolve, that too may change. Never miss that communication timeline. Bring in other managers on your behalf when necessary.

5. *Communicate Compassionately:* Do not leave out the relational human aspect. Acknowledge *emotional* aspects that people may be experiencing and let them know everyone may be navigating different emotional responses at different times and that's OK. You will work through all of it together. Encourage them to be patient with themselves and each other, sensitive to one another, and supportive of the impact this situation may have on everyone. Offer encouragement each time before you leave the communication podium.

The magnitude or nature of disruption does not change the communication pillars. In times of celebration, it may be easier to execute. However, when something is easy, don't diminish its importance, and most certainly, be glad for it. I recently enjoyed the privilege of working with an MBA student who chose us to continue in partnership with because of the level of communication she experienced with us. It made for a mutually productive relationship that was well aligned in approach and execution.

There are times in our businesses when tragedy or crisis ushers itself in. Crisis is at the extreme end of the disruption scale, but if you learn to navigate that well as a leader, all else will be simple to lead through. Because we are in the business of people, we have had our fair share of tragedy and losses. Each time, we have walked through it together—death, marriage crisis, illness, car accidents, and so on—it reaches all of us over time. In the most heartbreaking of times, people have communicated that our company, our support, was a lifeline or place of sanctuary. That is Leading for Impact. That is influencing with integrity—people first, in value and in action.

Managing the COVID-19 crisis is an example we all can relate to. We adhered strictly to the communication principles daily. Our team extended that communication into the community as much as we could. Communication was our lifeline with our office in one location, our homes scattered across different states, while experiencing personal family tragedy and loss. We lived the reality of the chaos. We adhered to our values, accepted the financial impact early, and placed our efforts on our people.

I was in constant communication with federal, state, and local agencies, business partners, CEO groups, schools, and various business associations. I shared updates regularly and let my team know what resources we had and what our approach and action items were. My team was the priority, and I made sure that our overall well-being was cared for through daily meetings and team engagement, moments to enjoy sunshine, wellness initiatives, tailgating in our office parking lot, and so on. The human element carried our team through. Communication not only has the power to heal emotions surrounding disruption, but it also carries us above and beyond during extreme times.

Press In and Press On

At a time when our culture generally avoids what is uncomfortable, and is attracted to emotionally "safe" places, COVID-19 flipped everything on its head. The problem is that the shutdowns created a place of escape through lack of accountability, lack of responsibility, and an incredible steamrolling of ideas. In some ways, it magnified one's ability to avoid personal and professional development and responsibilities. In other ways, it abruptly ended people's livelihood and left them isolated.

Whatever the circumstances then, now, or in the future, we as leaders need to press in and forge forward, bringing our teams with us. That's how we get through every situation. In a world where it's habitual to just "Google" information, I would argue that growth and development require *real people*. Even if you could reason that the internet world has accurate, unbiased information, we need *people* to influence the emotion and the growth that doesn't come from knowledge alone. *Human connection and the application of knowledge rely on the wisdom of leadership.* Strong leaders discern when to step back, step beside, and step forward. Personal and professional development are forms of disruption, which emphasize the need to invest in yourself and others. Resilience and *excellence* in the face of disruption take endless practice. Being present, responsive, and available are nonnegotiable attributes in my leadership.

As an executive leader, I can't help but embrace disruption and find merit in it. There's so much going on in all of our lives, but we provide a place to come back to each day together and to work with excellence. We have the privilege of having a place where we remain a productive, influential part of society. We provide for ourselves, our families, and the community. We take responsibility in protecting our own dignity and worth. We carry a lot in our lives, and it's natural to become depleted and disengaged, but every day presents the opportunity to press through, grow, and ultimately advance ourselves and our teams toward limitless potential.

Disruption hits all of us at the core. We are humans with profound emotions. As a leader, you should channel emotions in the right direction, but once again, it is best done while anchoring into those values. There are days you'll be upset or stressed, maybe momentarily defeated even. If you're rooted in your core principles, you can adapt to any situation, regardless of your personal state of mind, and weather the storm.

The best antidote to disruption is outward focus and engagement. Remembering the opportunity your role affords is to influence others with integrity—to show them how to walk the walk, to show them why value pillars are important and useful. Tempering your emotion fosters a safe place for your team. This doesn't mean you can't ever show your frustration or pretend nothing wrong ever happens; it just means that you need to set a stable pattern that invites people to come to you, regardless of the situation.

You are responsible for establishing trust. For me and my team, it's important to me that my staff feels supported and able to fail without fear. We establish efforts of excellence but agree to allow for stumbling and not kick each other while we are down. It's an incredible team effort to ensure that we can approach every situation in a positive light and even with some laughter.

Overall wellness is a growing concern. And as we commit to sharpening our discernment as leaders and successfully leading through disruption, the overall wellness of our teams will be lifted and protected. We are in a time of constant disruption, Leading for Impact calls upon us to hold the torch and keep it lit for ourselves and our teams.

Discerning Disruption

Discerning leaders navigate disruptions well and enable their teams to thrive.

SPARKS OF TRUTH

- A leader's impact is significant in times of uncertainty and disruption.

- Leaders are called to be vigilant, alert, and responsive.

- In the face of rapid change, there's one thing that we can control: *how we lead.*

- Human connection and the *application* of knowledge rely on the wisdom of leadership.

PROMPTS FOR IMPACT

- Identify the most urgent disruption impacting your business/team. How will you navigate through it successfully?

- What do you want people to see from you in times of opposition and controversy? And in times of celebration?

- How will you reshape communication within your company?

NOTES

....

....

....

....

....

....

....

....

....

....

....

....

....

....

I've made my share
of mistakes along
the way, but if I have
changed even one
life for the better, I
haven't lived in vain.

—MUHAMMAD ALI

CHAPTER EIGHT

Reshaping the Battle

reshape: to shape again or into a different form.

battle: to work very hard or strive; accomplish or struggle tenaciously to achieve or resist something.

Louis Armstrong's classic song, "What a Wonderful World," comes to mind when reshaping any battle. His vocals beautifully lift the positive lyrics of this song. It's the "*look-up* concept" I communicate to my team, epitomized in a melody we'll never forget. If you look down, the world closes in, but if you look up, the expanse of the sky symbolizes limitless opportunity.

We face so many battles in life, and even *achieving success* itself is a battle. You'll recall from Discerning Disruption that struggle is inevitable and even fruitful. Battles cultivate resilience, growth, and fortitude. Leaders with the proper attitude and mindset can reshape anything into a positive force for change, befitting this wonderful world:

I see trees of green
Red roses too
I see them bloom
For me and you
And I think to myself
What a wonderful world

I see skies of blue
And clouds of white
The bright blessed day
The dark sacred night
And I think to myself
What a wonderful world

The colors of the rainbow
So pretty in the sky
Are also on the faces
Of people going by

I see friends shaking hands
Saying, "How do you do?"
They're really saying
I love you

I hear babies cry
I watch them grow
They'll learn much more
Than I'll ever know

And I think to myself
What a wonderful world

Yes, I think to myself
What a wonderful world

**—"What a Wonderful World"
by Louis Armstrong**

Leading for Impact requires seeing things from different perspectives. The highest moment for you can be an intensely low one for someone else, and the valleys of your life may be exactly what you need to later summit the mountain top. Battles are both wins and losses because there is always another side to them that you aren't experiencing firsthand. When you're winning, someone else is losing—while you naturally sit on the side of elation. It takes intention to be aware of who is around you and include them in the celebration—to acknowledge with humility that there are others sitting in a less fortunate seat, one *you too* have sat in more than a time or two. Don't forget those moments. No one wins alone.

I watched a lot of football growing up. I'm sure you can relate to the absolute jubilation when your team wins the Super Bowl! The moment is spectacular, and then there's the losing team, offsetting the heights of winning, in the depths of defeat. It's always interesting to witness the reporter trying to capture those raw moments from the athletes in that heightened moment, both from those who have won and from those who have lost.

Part of me is always thinking, "Give them their moment to take it in, to reset, whether in jubilation or defeat." Any "battle" or circumstance can carry deep emotion on both sides, but we reshape it when we realize that it's not just about us ("me"). When you win, acknowledge those who got you there. When you lose, be grateful for the experience that will refine your next steps. *The battle isn't just about you, and a broader lens helps you to appreciate that all battles have a bigger meaning and purpose.*

The Winning Lens

In many respects, winners and losers are the same because they both showed up, and they both must navigate the outcome. I'm not advocating the "everyone gets a trophy" concept—someone outperformed, out-practiced, outwitted, and out-passioned another, and someone else lost. Having said that, a worthy opponent makes a victory sweeter, and losing to a worthy opponent can lessen the sting of defeat. Most of us are not *given* anything in life—we *get* to compete. Competition is not a barrier; it's a means to succeed. Reshaping any battle means you've shown up to engage, work hard, and win.

Let's come back to that infamous song by Louis Armstrong. The song was released in 1967 during the controversial Vietnam War, and because it wasn't promoted by the studio, it was more popular abroad than at home. It gained popularity in the United States years later after making the soundtrack for the film *Good Morning, Vietnam*. Today, it continues to be a much loved, heartwarming anthem enjoyed by many all over the world.

The depth of simple words and one of the most notable voices of all time seems to just lift people out of their difficult circumstances, even if for a moment. Armstrong used a beautiful gift of talent to establish a legacy that would leave a profound impact on future generations. Conflict and challenges are present at any given moment in life; you need only wake each morning to find them. What matters more are the refinements and new victories that result from those very battles and the opportunities for lasting impact.

I'll be a bit blunt. Circumstances and people can suck. If you examine any situation and seek out the "yuck" factor, you'll find it without a doubt. If you're looking for ugliness and imperfections, you don't have to look too hard, long, or far. However, with intention, we teach ourselves to seek out through a different lens—one that exudes positivity, rather than sinks in the spoils of humanity. The beauty of "What a Wonderful World" is the simplicity of seeing the world through a different lens than the negative reality that may exist at any given time.

This skill is a mindset that must be exercised. It's too easy to sit in idleness, opine, or complain. As I wake each morning, I begin with gratitude for a new day—whatever it holds—and for the breath of life I can so easily take for granted. When I lay my head down at night to fall asleep, I pray with the same heart of gratitude yet also a repentant heart for my wrongdoings that I may not have caught during that day, and further gratitude for the blessings of the day, including the fact that I survived. Not everyone is promised the gift of a new day and a time to rest, and I don't ever wish to take that for granted. This is my way of reshaping my mind every day in readiness for new battles.

We win and we lose, but more importantly, we're all in a state of grace. Each of us owns our plentiful share of mistakes, but so also do we have a chance to do good, to be better, and to make someone else better, too. We each can carry a heart of gratitude into every battle and be intentional about reshaping it. You alone have the power to choose which lens you look through that you intentionally bring into focus each day. There are so many dark trails any one of us can go down—we are given free will to choose our own adventure. I choose to *look up*.

Such a simple practice. Look up, and see the sunrise, sunsets, stars, and rainbows—every day and night, it's there for us. This truth taught me a lot about reshaping the battle every day. None of this splendor costs us a thing and is so uplifting to the spirit. During a personal battle, you can still recall wonderful things people have said and done and how they've enriched your life. You can find gratitude in what people do, and even if someone does something terribly wrong, there's always hope to be found in reconciliation or on the other side of the hurt.

The battle can be anything, to any given person, any given day—different for each of us. Daily life annoyances like allergies, car issues, and so on, whatever it is, you can flip it and find a way to be grateful. Leading for Impact requires reshaping your mindset. It means approaching the small struggles just as you would the big ones—with the intent of moving forward.

Villains and Victors

Intention also brings us to the notion that, in life, there are villains and victors. Both arrive there as a positive or a negative consequence of their actions or inactions. It involves intentional choice and effort. A villain chooses their own action and creates their place. The same goes for the victor—it's a choice and result of one's actions.

If you don't actively choose victory, you're passively choosing a different path. It's not active, but it still is a choice. You're culpable on that path that compels you toward destructive consequences. *Leaders don't always go down the wrong path with full awareness, but intentionality is what gets you out of it.* I'm reminded of the words of Muhammad Ali. He once said, "Inside of a ring or out, ain't nothing wrong with going down. It's *staying* down that's wrong." Leaders are not void of mistakes, but they bear the responsibility to correct those missteps. You do, in fact, *choose* the path of victory.

There's a fundamental importance to the timing of what you do, the intention behind it, and how you choose to act to reshape that battle. Whether you're standing still, moving forward, or stepping backward, leaders must step in and do the heavy lifting. Yes, that's a lot of responsibility to put on a person who didn't invent a situation, but that's also the responsibility you take on as you step into a leadership role. You don't necessarily get to pick your battles. Often even, your team, your clients, and the world pick them for you. Let your values guide you to victory. Leading for Impact calls upon you to be the victor.

Victor's Enemy

The leaders' circle, the journey of a victor, is not a stranger to fear. *Fear* is such a little word, yet it will take whatever power you are willing to give to it. Given the freedom, it can manifest itself through anxiety, apprehension, despair, doubt, panic, worry, dread, and all things immobilizing and defeating. Understanding your fear and disarming it are essential to reshaping it.

Fear is the enemy to forward. Fear is not a friend to progress. Fear can't heal your soul. Fear is a robber of joy, strips away potential, and projects negative outcomes as the only reality. Even for the greatest of fears in life—whatever they are to you—the remedy is always for you to take action. All crises are intensified by fear. Merely showing up speaks volumes. The fact that you are willing to be present, with the right or wrong words but the best *intentions*, evidences that the battle is already being reshaped by your action. Your very presence and intention can be transformative.

Fear preys on the ill-informed and can be self-consuming. Imagine not having all the information necessary to make a decision, to rationalize your position, understanding, and defense. It's difficult, if not impossible, to reshape something in a beneficial way without accurate knowledge and experience. In our modern world, this might even be fear caused by what is being fed to us, what we're choosing to consume, where we are gathering our news, and whom we allow to influence us. How much time you spend doing independent research, deductive reasoning, critical thinking, and problem-solving for yourself—all of this has bearing on the level of fear that creeps its way in to our days.

In my audit, ministry, consulting, and recruiting experiences, I've been taught to observe with a critical eye and ask open-ended questions. A discerning spirit also helps sift through the answers and navigate truth. Fear breeds on lack of information or the *right* information. As you take charge and do your own sifting, fear tends to dissipate. The world can overwhelm us if we let it. The way information is delivered, the amount of information, and the information we already have can create tremendous fear. Whatever we receive, as devastating as it might be, can be reshaped through action and our own resolve. The same fear you invite is the same fear you have the ability to remove.

Battle's Opportunity

Reshaping the battle, whether circumstance, people, or fear—looking at it from all angles and seeking solutions—changes *you*. Some battles are simply meant to make us stronger, and it inevitably has reshaped *us* as a company. The emphasis on values has never been lost in the disruptions and battles that came our way. In fact, they were what defined who we were (and still are) and shaped how we respond(ed) in battle. I am pleased to share a couple of excerpts of internal communications from me to my staff, which evidences our commitment to living our values—the core of who we are:

March 12, 2020

This week in particular has been a week of unprecedented accelerating in government-mandated action for our community, and there is undeniably more to come. Therefore, it is wise for us to take notice of what is happening around us in our community at large. Our values define us and right now it's time for us to honor our commitment to serve our community generously. It normally means we should go out and do, but who would have guessed it could also mean stay in and do not? Tomorrow, we will conduct our morning meeting, as normal, and then I would like you to gather what you need to work remote ... As inconvenient as this may be, remember that it is also a privilege that some cannot even afford to offer.

This is a time for us to be generous with what we have and what we are able to do (or not do). If you are blessed with health and a secure job (as we are), it's a good time to think of those who are not in such a state of security. Lives are being disrupted and we count our blessings that we are able to take a sideline view right now. But, find a way to step onto the field and give. Give in your own way. Be a positive ripple in a lake filled with uncertainty.

Rest well. Smile when you wake up in the Morning. Stay Awesome.

As the lockdowns ensued for much longer in our area, I continued to act on concern for our employees, and in July 2020, in the midst of a family emergency, I issued a Team Wellness Incentive Program:

> The success of our company is a reflection of our team. The ability to foster meaningful relationships depends on the overall well-being of our people. 2020 is a uniquely challenging year and every dimension of who we are seems to be vulnerable. Yet, we set our values down as a firm foundation, and even as we display humility in all things, we must also be mindful that the integrity we committed to is hinged on fortitude. So, through adversity and struggle—through 2020—we will rise up, as a team, to meet each challenge and uphold all the principles core to who we are.
>
> Wellness is caring for ourselves in order that we may care well for others—impact. This takes awareness and deliberate effort to achieve a healthy, purposed, and fulfilling life. I invite you to truly elevate your potential through intentional care for every aspect of you: spiritual, emotional, intellectual, physical, relational—however you define each part of who you are—Dignity.

Words like *disruption* and *battle* aren't anyone's favorite, but these circumstances present tremendous opportunity. Every battle, every challenge or dip in your business, is actually a blessing when you view it as offering another perspective and another opportunity to show who you are. *When you build a habit of reshaping your battles, the fruit is the character refinement that the experience instills in you.* All you have to remember in this wonderful world is to "look up."

Reshaping the Battle

Leaders with proper attitude and mindset can reshape anything into a positive force for change.

SPARKS OF TRUTH

- Leading for Impact requires seeing things from different perspectives.

- All battles have a bigger meaning and purpose.

- Competition is not a barrier; it's a means to success.

- Victory is a choice.

- Understanding your fear and disarming it are essential to reshaping it.

PROMPTS FOR IMPACT

- What battle is at the forefront of your mind right now? How will you reshape it in positive, refining action?

- Where are you acting as a villain? How will you transform that to a victor?

- What fear(s) of yours can you name? How will you disarm it (them)?

NOTES

....

....

....

....

....

....

....

....

....

....

....

....

....

....

....

As we express our gratitude, we must never forget that the highest appreciation is not to utter words, but to live by them.

—JOHN F. KENNEDY

CHAPTER NINE

Celebrate Generously

celebrate: acknowledge or make known publicly; commemorate with ceremonies or festivities.

generously: abundant; free from meanness or smallness of mind or character; unselfish.

February 2, 2014—the Seattle Seahawks versus the Denver Broncos. Super Bowl XLVIII. The Seahawks crushed the Broncos 43–8, the largest margin of victory for an underdog in Super Bowl history. Celebrating generously means sharing in victories and celebrating others. Indeed, I and millions of other fans did celebrate that Seahawks' victory in *community*. There was electricity in the air. You could feel it. It was contagious! Everyone has these moments in life—in sports, academia, philanthropy, personal milestones, and life events—times that are deeply meaningful and memorable to you. Whatever it is, big or small, we should count ourselves fortunate to have and share in an experience of such elation.

As a big Seahawks fan, my mind screamed, SUPER BOWL CHAMPIONS! I remember not wanting to go to sleep that night. It felt like I somehow had won a championship, too! The enthusiasm and joy were overwhelming. Strangers hugged strangers and jumped around like foolish kids with not a care in the world. The snow fell late that night, and it may as well have been confetti in my memory. As we celebrated in Times Square, we watched the entire state of Washington celebrate with us!

True story, we were the first flight home the next day, with *the Hawk*, our mascot, on board. No one could prepare us for what awaited us—it was a massive surprise. There was a crowd at the gate to welcome us home—balloons, reporters, chanting—I didn't even know who these people were or how they got there, but they made that moment incredible! They followed us all to baggage claim and just kept the celebration going. In fact, the jubilation for the community carried on straight through to the following season. I'll never forget it (I honestly don't know who really won, the players or the fans!). Life certainly offers us beautiful moments to celebrate.

In business, we don't have these over-the-top moments every day, and perhaps not necessarily at this scale, but we do have victories and people who should be celebrated. At Summit Group, we are *intentional* and *sacrificial* about taking those moments to honor each new team member, acknowledge performance achievements, celebrate birthdays, work anniversaries, and so on. We build gratitude for what we do, how we do it, and who does it. Every person and every role are essential—none more important than another.

Yes, individual accolades are necessary, but we, as a *team*, share in the victories and in the mistakes. Our team's vision is to give generously. The work that we do—showing up and working hard to make a living—enables us to give back, each in ways meaningful to us individually. Every day presents an opportunity to show up for someone else and make them feel a sense of belonging and appreciation. It doesn't have to be done on a grand scale; it needs to just be genuine. This mindset—celebrating big and small victories with others—will transform your culture and your business.

Victory's Moments

If I had a superpower, it would be Marvel's Time Stone keeper. I could preserve, relive, and revisit moments that have meaning—graduation, first job, paying off student loans and being debt-free (for a hot second!), engagement, moments in faith, marriage, the births of my children, one of the last memories of my mom at Christmas, getting my first puppy (then the second and third), and so on. What does your list look like? Possibly for most, if not many, the top-of-mind things are personal life imprints and *big* life milestones. Those indeed are special and anchor themselves in our memories. Think of the emotions and feelings surrounding those moments—that's what we want to harness and release into our "everyday littles"—small bursts of confetti, with lasting impact.

There are moments in life that are so special that we want to cling to them. However, if we allow ourselves to dwell in or hold tightly to the past, we will miss the abundance that each day has to offer. If we live in and build gratitude for life, there will never be a shortage of people and things that bring joy to our lives, in and out of work. Look for the little winning moments of the day: *Woke up to the sunrise, hit all the green traffic lights, received a text from _____, had the best coffee, a stranger said, "Good morning," my desk was clean.* The list should be bountiful and endless. Every day, I open my eyes and am thankful that it's a new day because I get to start over. *I get a do-over today, to do better.*

At Summit Group, living in humility and gratitude is part of our culture. It's what we teach, appreciate, and expect. Our values and vision aren't just marketing words we've written on our website; it is what we do, and it is how we work. This past year, we invested in an engagement platform that helps us make known the good things, the *impact*, that other people are making. It's a way to celebrate them by commending these individuals on how they upheld specific values. Our corporate values guide us to:

APPRECIATE IMPACT

Grasp onto the value that others bring to your workday. Grow in gratitude for your team and the value each person contributes.

NOTICE THE MOMENTS

Teach yourself to acknowledge and articulate the contributions of others. Broaden your perspective beyond yourself, as this promotes a selfless mindset.

BE THE INITIATOR

Build in a practice of showing up to encourage and affirm others. This gives everyone the opportunity to lead out in a positive, affirming way.

EXPERIENCE TOGETHER

Experiences done together bond people together. Celebrating others fosters a culture of gratitude for each other.

TEACH OTHERS TO RECIPROCATE

Modeling how to live out your values and celebrate others generously starts with you as a leader. Teach them, show them, and then let them become the teacher for others.

REPEAT

Do this daily. There isn't a shortage of opportunity. *Live* it.

Leading for Impact means working on and building contentment. Happiness is fleeting, but contentment is lasting. Creating a grateful heart and forming a positive mindset set a formidable tone as you navigate through a rapidly changing world. Name your values that are at the core of your team; start small, and intentionally celebrate little moments every day.

There are always things that will go wrong, and they have a way of getting your attention. Your leadership is valuable in reshaping those "less than" moments and repurposing them to point back to lessons in continual development and harnessing appreciation, whatever the circumstance. Reshaping our battles, discerning disruption, and actively moving everyone toward humility and gratitude make celebrating simple.

Thoughtful Impact

Gratitude and appreciation are transformative. Summit Group's key performance indicators and metrics provide us with a road map of things to celebrate, spotting the small victories, as well as the big wins. How people show up for their jobs, what they do for others, and how they stretch beyond their roles present a picture of the internal state of the culture.

For me, I am truly blessed to have such a generous team. If I've been coughing, I'll find a glass of water or a cup of tea on my desk. Once, I arrived in town for a quick trip and noticed how clean everything was. The team made sure to tidy up and wipe everything down to welcome me. Another time, I was in town for a conference, and someone on our team dropped off some tea, bananas, and waffles at my hotel because they knew I was exhausted and would skip breakfast. One night they all joined me for dinner, even though, for some of them, it wasn't their restaurant of choice. We had such a fun time together nonetheless.

Fridays, we typically work from home, so when I was in town, I didn't want to disrupt that. However, knowing I was in person, they all showed up at the office—every single one of them. When we need a team break or when we celebrate someone, everyone is quick to come to the table and bring fun ideas and execution with them. Each one of them brings treats in for everyone to share—they are a thoughtful bunch. *Those* are the moments that matter, that make us work harder for each other. Those are the pieces of each person that we want to celebrate.

Thoughtful actions are shout-outs from your culture. It's the outworking of the kindness and generosity that we learn to celebrate every day within our walls. Inevitably, it cannot be contained. It is authentic and overflows in all that we do.

Contagious Gratitude

Leading for Impact doesn't follow the same paradigm as other leadership models. We're not defining success along the revenue line. It's not about what we have but what we have to *give (our vision statement)*. Our values bring fulfillment to our jobs. My fellow editors on this book have argued that I'm the one who has created contagious gratitude in our culture, but I'd beg to differ. Celebration comes from *all* of us as a team, and it's appreciated by those who share in the same values or learn to appreciate who we are at our core. It's funny looking back. What our team shares today is beyond any team as a whole that came before. We have reached a point where everyone on the team authentically lives out who we are together.

Summit Group's values and vision have been a game changer for our team *and* our business. Not because they are especially unique but because there is community buy-in and evidence of it from the whole team, consistently. It's the core of who we are and how we approach our work. There's a huge leap in mentality from "We're forced to work with these people" to "This is our team." I get to choose the team, but the team members don't always choose each other. They land together. Even with our diverse group of personalities, contagious gratitude keeps us together. It's the glue that binds us.

This is a time of great enjoyment for me, when I can fully give and be generous, not having to withhold because someone isn't toeing the line. Our team comes from different backgrounds, experiences, opinions, and personalities, but our core values unify us. We have the freedom to be ourselves uniquely while operating with a common core. It encourages us to be generous with our time, talents, and gratitude toward each other.

Gift-Giver

Leading for Impact requires an intentional change in perspective. It's a *choice* and a practice to celebrate generously. Know what the other person appreciates, and celebrate them in *their* way, without any expectation of gaining something in return. Knowing about the other person (being interested in them) is essential to create meaningful moments for them. This is the purest giving—sacrificial giving.

I have been taught a great lesson in how affection grows when you give to another person. I am convinced that this is where "'tis better to give than to receive" found its origins. Our culture teaches us to focus on the recipient, but it's really the *giver* who provides the lesson. Rabbi Daniel Lapin states, "Ancient Jewish wisdom explains that when one person transfers something material to another, paradoxically, the giver tends to gain more affection for the recipient than the other way around."

To build on this, there's a famous quote in Benjamin Franklin's biography where he describes not being liked (essentially dismissed) by an older member of the Pennsylvania House. He famously said, "I did not aim at gaining his favor by paying any servile respect to him but took this other method."[2] Franklin ended up borrowing his rival's book (on loan), only to leave a letter of appreciation inside. The two became friends for life. This makes sense. According to Rabbi Daniel

---

2   Benjamin Franklin, "The Autobiography of Benjamin Franklin," USHistory.org, Independence Hall Association, accessed May 30, 2023, https://www.ushistory.org/franklin/autobiography/page48.htm.

Lapin, "Once we've given a gift or done a favor for someone, we experience a subconscious tendency to like that person."[3]

Begin by just the action of giving, and then pay attention as your affection for that person blossoms. You have created a bond through giving. At this point, your generosity is intentional. I see this in situations with someone who may not find a connection with me or whom I wouldn't necessarily get along with. I intentionally seek to find common ground and focus on that. It's amazing to see how the unlikeliness of connection melts away and mutual affection and celebration are established.

You, as the giver, experience incredible joy when you receive back from someone you've grown to like. What's more is that you've created a heart for giving in yourself and taught someone else how to give. The relational piece is magnified when both parties are engaged in giving and receiving. Sacrificial giving—this is what brings people together in a diverse world. It will also bring your team together.

---

3   Rabbi Daniel Lapin, "Some Give and Take," RabbiDanielLapin.com, accessed May 30, 2023, https://rabbidaniellapin.com/some-give-and-take/.

Celebrate Generously

CHAPTER SPOTLIGHT

Celebrating generously means acknowledging others and celebrating them in abundance, without expectation of anything in return.

SPARKS OF TRUTH

- Every day presents an opportunity to show up for someone else.

- Your leadership is valuable in reshaping those "less than" moments.

- Gratitude and appreciation are transformative.

- Thoughtful actions are "shout-outs" from your corporate culture.

PROMPTS FOR IMPACT

- You get a do-over today. What will you do better?

- What are your little winning moments of today?

- What do the "shout-outs" you observe say about your corporate culture?

NOTES

....

....

....

....

....

....

....

....

....

....

....

....

....

....

....

We can't help everyone,
but everyone can
help someone.

—RONALD REAGAN

CHAPTER TEN

Elevate Your Impact

elevate: raise the spirits of; move to a higher position; fill with great joy.

impact: have a strong effect on someone or something.

Elevating your impact magnifies how you serve others with the intention of leaving a lasting impression of joy or raising their spirits in a genuine manner. It begins with you as a leader—how you show up each day, what you do, and your heart-attitude evidenced in action. It's fostering relationships and making a positive impression where you lead and where you are led to. This is a high calling. It comes with the privilege of leading others. You have to stand in constant readiness, knowing that you have the potential to impact others in big and small ways.

Leading for Impact, *elevating your impact*, puts the best interests of others first—setting yourself aside, your fears, insecurities, pride, and selfish desires. It's serving and not self-serving. *Humility.* The purpose intended for you is bigger than yourself; it is made for having others in mind. Summit Group's vision statement is, "We measure success not by what we have, but by what we have to give." This is loosely based on a Winston Churchill quote: "We make a living by what we get, but we make a life by what we give." Our impact is outward-facing, and it calls for us to move ourselves aside and focus on how we show up for other people—at home, at work, and in our communities.

That's the essence of elevating your impact. *You can make a lot of money, or own a lot of possessions, but all of this is meaningless if you're not serving out your purpose and doing something with what you're given in life.* Purpose gives meaning, and meaning breeds impact. So, what is *your* purpose? Summit Group is not solely focused on staffing and recruiting. That is our core business, but it is not our core purpose. Not only do we strive to give back to the community, but our "work" is also about developing ourselves to be effective vessels with a broader reach. Our team is devoted to a variety of charities and networking relationships, but our passion has to authentically start individually, showing up at our best in every aspect of our lives, wherever we choose to put our time and effort.

My own purpose demands meaningful intention. Every part of my day, and whatever I've been given, has been purposed to equip me to be the best steward over those I am accountable to and what I am responsible for. That's how you elevate your impact, with meaningful intention—well-purposed, well-practiced, and well-prepared effort to accomplish whatever is set before you.

You'll recall from chapter 1, The Leader You Are, that bringing your full self in an undivided, honest way is the key to authentically bringing your best self *completely* to each new situation. Devote yourself to constant learning and development so that you don't become a stumbling block or bottleneck to those you lead. You can't take people further than you've gone yourself. A leader should never be the one lagging behind. Set the pace, stay ahead, and be challenged from those sprinting to pass you. When you give and serve with excellence, you lead for impact.

Forever Journey

Leading for Impact is a constant journey. There's never a stopping point. *The only means to elevate our impact is to be a forever learner, teacher, and giver.* Not until my very last breath will I stop on the path set for me. Part of my appreciation for those whom I have poured into is that they've supported me in turn. That's what keeps my feet moving and never idle. A leader who influences with integrity will never cease to serve *others* in truth, and with their best interests in mind. Humility and gratitude are components of this ever-flowing practice—never becoming so arrogant as to think you've "arrived." There isn't a finish line. Never lose sight of those who came before, who walk with you presently, and who will be there on the path you have yet to reach.

So much of our continuous growth comes from understanding ourselves and working with who we are. I've come a long way on the road to compassion. I was highly self-protective and independent growing up because of my home life. Coming to grips with this in adulthood, I concluded that there was a lot of *I* involved. My focus on personal growth led to the realization that we're naturally designed to be in a community with *others*. We're supposed to trust other people. Leading others helps you connect with a community, and the *people* in that community draw out compassion from you. Having people look to you for direction prompts your responsibility to grow in every way—knowledge, perspective, and character. You become responsible for *you* and accountable to others.

Progress is sometimes difficult to determine when you see all the demands upon you. You know where you've been, but there is always uncertainty in the road before you. The more you know, the more you realize what you don't know and how far you still have left to go. Life in business offers limitless travel destinations. The measure of how far you have come, how you are doing, is not up to your own biased assessment.

> A good name is more desirable than great riches; to be esteemed is better than silver or gold.
>
> **—Proverbs 22:1**

Listen well; observe well. Take your eyes from your own progress, and measure your devotion by the progress of those you lead. That is a stable and reliable measure of your leadership. Look to your advisors and mentors to guide and challenge you and also to commend you. Lean not on your own understanding or measure. Let it be evidenced all around you.

Establish a pattern, in all you do, that represents you. Let your actions and impact speak for themselves so that you need not utter a word in self-promotion. *Do what is right, be open to others, work hard—unceasingly—and live out your values.* These actions are what people see, and this is the evidence of growth. It extinguishes pride, makes way for gratitude, and perpetuates humility.

Elevate Others

In the spring of 2021, I was asked for a statement about what Summit Group does. I wrote, "We're here to support the creative brilliance that touches the lives of people and businesses across the globe." Elevating your impact as a leader extends beyond the business and connects with the people. Our mission is to unite talent and technology through relationship-focused staffing and recruiting solutions. That is what Summit Group Solutions does, but it doesn't capture *all* that we are. It doesn't capture *why* and *how* or the richness of our larger vision.

We are guiding, growing, and giving to the future of technology through people and relationships. Summit Group aims to be meaningful and impactful in and outside of business. *We have the privilege of investing in and elevating the talent that brings the unimaginable to fruition:*

- To our candidates, we offer to be a guide through their career and foster professional growth through engaging in the right opportunities. Our network is open to any candidate that connects with us, regardless of whether we receive a financial reward.

- To our clients, we partner in their business growth by bringing the best talent to deliver on their key initiatives. We establish open communication to support a mutually productive engagement. We believe in navigating success together.

- To our communities, we promise to serve with integrity and generosity, always giving back to the areas where we live and work. Whether in plenty or in want, we commit to investing our time, talents, and financial support into our communities.

Our commitment to elevating others comes from being guided by our core values and our vision. We value the worth of every person and are committed to honoring one another with kindness and respect. We value positive relationships in business and in the community. We are committed to using our individual gifts and talents to serve others generously. Elevating others is a critical part of Leading for Impact.

Do nothing out of selfish ambition or vain conceit. Rather, in humility value others above yourselves, not looking to your own interests but each of you to the interests of others.

—Philippians 2:3–4

Influence through Integrity

Integrity is unabashed honesty—understanding moral right and wrong. It's doing what's right all the time, even in the dark. Not for accolades or anything in return but behaving with integrity when no one is watching. It's that incorruptible spirit and sound judgment far too rare in business and the community at large today. Summit Group values humble fortitude—being void of pride and allowing the humility necessary to invite wisdom, which guides you to do what is right, even in or *especially* in the face of adversity in its many forms.

We're committed to living out our strong moral principles to uphold our reputation. I tell my team, "We all have our good days and our bad days." I have my bad days for sure! None of us has one perfect day. We stumble and we fall. We have grumpy moments. Elevating your impact means leaning into your humanity while committing to the refining fire. Raising the bar instead of asking for a free pass. Knowing when to extend grace and when to challenge yourself and your team to just do better. Striving for excellence every day and refusing to settle for mediocrity.

Integrity is found in every policy, process, and procedure we adhere to, and it's the constant pursuit of people who share our commitments. Influencing with integrity is holding yourself to the highest accountability, admitting when you are wrong, seeking reconciliation, and elevating others beyond yourself but never in conflict with the values that anchor you. *Elevating your impact is the culmination of who you are and what you have done thus far and then demanding more.*

Elevate Your Impact

Elevating your impact magnifies who you are and how well you serve others.

SPARKS OF TRUTH

- Leaders stand in constant readiness, knowing that you have the potential to impact others in big and small ways.

- Devote yourself to constant learning and development so that you don't become a stumbling block or bottleneck to those you lead.

- Elevating your impact means leaning into your humanity while committing to the refiner's fire.

- Influencing with integrity is holding to the values that anchor you.

PROMPTS FOR IMPACT

- How does your leadership show your own constant readiness for the opportunity to impact others?

- What area of self-development are you committed to right now? Share your approach, struggles, and progress.

NOTES

....

....

....

....

....

....

....

....

....

....

....

....

....

....

At the end of the day, it's not about what you have or even what you've accomplished. It's about what you've done with those accomplishments. It's about who you've lifted up, who you've made better. It's about what you've given back.

—DENZEL WASHINGTON

CONCLUSION

impact: my sign off and your new journey.

This is where my influence ends and your story begins. The "final chapter," this last part, is written by *you*, for your own journey. It is a launching pad from the pages of this book into your growth and commitment as a leader. Your leadership begins with who you are and how you relate to others. Define who you are as a person and as a leader—that is your foundation. Embrace your own unique purpose, and use it to serve others generously. Leading for Impact and influencing with integrity are now your privilege to carry out. Congratulations, now set your vision in motion.

Thank you for joining me on this journey. May your intentional efforts in personal and professional development transcend your leadership and transform those you lead and serve.

Leadership Launching Plan Idea Sheet

LEADERSHIP SPOTLIGHT:

Develop a purpose statement that gives meaning to your leadership.

LEADERSHIP VALUES:

List three to five values that define you as a leader.

LEADERSHIP PRINCIPLES:

List one to three principles or pillars that are important for your business. Connect them with your values.

LEADERSHIP DEVELOPMENT PLAN:

List up to three leadership development prompts to focus on in the next six months. Commit to a plan, an accountability partner, and what success looks like.

Leading for Impact: The CEO's Guide to Influencing with Integrity

- **The Leader You Are**

  Use your authority and influence for a positive purpose.

- **Confident Humility**

  Show confidence in holding a balanced opinion of one's self.

- **Servant Warrior**

  Be a brave, trustworthy leader who serves others.

- **Relational Relevance**

  Make meaningful connections and keep people "top of mind."

- **Leading Sacrificially**

  Serve others through sacrificial means.

- **Open-Handed Embrace**

  Give of yourself generously to support another.

- **Discerning Disruption**

  Sense disruptions and navigate them well.

- **Reshaping the Battle**

  Hold a proper attitude and mindset to reshape anything into a positive force.

- **Celebrate Generously**

  Acknowledge others and celebrate them generously.

- **Elevate Your Impact**

  Magnify how you serve others with positive intention.

Whatever you do, work at it with all your heart, as working for the Lord, not for human masters.

—COLOSSIANS 3:23NIV

ABOUT THE AUTHOR

The call to leadership is a lesson in humility and gratitude. It's the willingness and commitment to serve others with a grateful heart. Opportunities for leading others surround us at every stage of our lives. I believe in embracing those opportunities and upholding each role with integrity.

My life purpose is to be a faithful steward over all that God has entrusted to me. This has encouraged me to fearlessly surrender myself every day to whatever the cause set before me. Thirty years of professional field experience, including twenty years of devoted life-on-life ministry, have led me to become the cofounder and CEO of Summit Group Solutions, LLC, 2023 Inc. Power Partner, CyberReadyMBE designated, and a multi-year Inc. 5000 awardee. We unite talent and technology in support of the creative brilliance that touches the lives of people and businesses across the globe.

The shared vision we have as a company measures success by what we *give*. We value positive relationships in business and in the community. We are committed to using our gifts and talents to be the hands and feet that serve others generously where we live and work.

I admire people with courage, reasoning minds, useful hands, servant's feet, and humble spirits.

CONTACT PAGE

To explore more about Summit Group Solutions, go to:
www.summitgroupsolutions.com.

To contact Jennifer Schielke regarding speaking engagements, training, or consulting, please connect at:
www.linkedin.com/in/jenniferschielke.

ACKNOWLEDGMENTS

Thank you to my husband, Bryan, who supported my career and devotion to ministry, allowing me the freedom to soar. The founding of Summit Group Solutions, LLC was his vision that I was merely invited into.

To my children whose hearts are devoted to God and continue to grow in faith: I am so proud of you and the ways that you serve your community. You will each be an incredible blessing to this world.

Leila, your laughter is my joy. Your talents are limitless. Thank you for inspiring the cover design and for your encouragement throughout each stage of this book.

TJ, you are wise beyond your years, witty without effort, and a leader in the making.

To my parents. Through struggles and hardship, you gave me the love you had to spare, taught me to earn my way without excuses, and encouraged me to forge my own path. To my late mother, I am blessed to have gained your smile, tolerance, and strength that was seldom credited your way.

All employees past, present, and future of Summit Group Solutions, LLC: thank you for the lovely ride, for being part of my growth, and for being willing to take a chance on the small and mighty sitting among the giants. May our company continue to be a sanctuary, a stepping stone, and a career home that enriches the lives of our employees and their families.

How blessed is one person who has a list such as this: Amy, Annabelle, Anne, Britt, Debra, Elizabeth, Emily, Gina, Jennifer N., Jennifer T., Kelley, Maile, Norma, and Suzie. Thank you for your generous friendship and support through the years.

To the team at Advantage Media Group and Forbes Books, thank you for being there every step of the way to bring this book to fruition. These pages are a reflection of your encouragement and guidance. I learned so much about publishing and am grateful to have been surrounded by the best in the business!

NOTES

....
....
....
....
....
....
....
....
....
....
....
....
....
....
....

NOTES

NOTES

....
....
....
....
....
....
....
....
....
....
....
....
....
....

NOTES

....

....

....

....

....

....

....

....

....

....

....

....

....

....

Printed in the USA
CPSIA information can be obtained
at www.ICGtesting.com
JSHW022025051223
53317JS00001B/1